TWAYNE'S WORLD AUTHORS SERIES

A Survey of the World's Literature

Sylvia E. Bowman, Indiana University

GENERAL EDITOR

GERMAN LITERATURE

Ulrich Weisstein, Indiana University

EDITOR

Nikolaus Lenau

(TWAS 135)

TWAYNE'S WORLD AUTHORS SERIES (TWAS)

The purpose of TWAS is to survey the major writers —novelists, dramatists, historians, poets, philosophers, and critics—of the nations of the world. Among the national literatures covered are those of Australia, Canada, China, Eastern Europe, France, Germany, Greece, India, Italy, Japan, Latin America, New Zealand, Poland, Russia, Scandinavia, Spain, and the African nations, as well as Hebrew, Yiddish, and Latin Classical literatures. This survey is complemented by Twayne's United States Authors Series and English Authors Series.

The intent of each volume in these series is to present a critical-analytical study of the works of the writer; to include biographical and historical material that may be necessary for understanding, appreciation, and critical appraisal of the writer; and to present all material in clear, concise English—but not to vitiate the scholarly content of the work by doing so.

Nikolaus Lenau

By HUGO SCHMIDT
University of Colorado

Twayne Publishers, Inc. :: New York

Library of Congress Catalog Card Number: 68-17227

MANUFACTURED IN THE UNITED STATES OF AMERICA

To

Professor Walter Silz

Preface

In literary history, Nikolaus Lenau has suffered the fate of one who owed his initial fame to a fashion. To his own and several subsequent generations, he was the poet of *Weltschmerz.* His early readers were enchanted by the melancholy atmosphere of his poems and consumed them with more regard to the realm into which his verse transported them than to the verse itself. By the time the *Weltschmerz* movement had ceased to be a fashion and the readers of poetic best sellers were looking to be transported to other realms, Lenau was laid aside as dated. Even literary history is slow to reinstate one whose fame stood on grounds that proved to be unstable. More recently, Lenau has been rediscovered by critics with an interest in existential philosophy, so that currently he and his works are riding a second wave of fashion.

This study will examine Lenau's work as poetic art, and not primarily as the mouthpiece of a spiritual or cultural movement. Although many of Lenau's poems may have lost some of the impact they had on the age for which they were written, others are of lasting value. In this book, criteria will be established to assess Lenau's permanent achievement and to distinguish the subtle layers of his poetic imagination. A fresh, if cursory, look will be taken at his life as well, mostly in order to dispel that old fallacy in Lenau criticism which equates the poet's art with his life.

Since the work of a lyric poet cannot be discussed without attention to linguistic details, we shall quote liberally from Lenau's works. And since the choice of the individual word, its associations, its sound, and the rhythmic cadence of the line and stanza are primary constituents in the art of poetry, these quotations will appear in the original. It was difficult to decide what aids should be offered to the reader who has little or no knowledge of German. English verse translations of a good many of Lenau's poems do exist and could have been used, so that our choice of plain prose renditions may require a word of justification.

To translate a poem from one language into another is a

relatively futile endeavor. The language of poetry is compact, rich in overtones, radiant in connotations and tonal beauty. No two languages are alike in the means by which a poet can create this effect. If a poetic translation is attempted by a competent linguist, it will not thereby become a poem; if it is undertaken by another poet, it will become a different poem. Yet the reader, faced with a poetic translation, will not easily resist the temptation of taking it for the real thing. On the other hand, if he is offered a stubbornly modest prose rendition, he will remain aware of the original and look to it in search of the poetry which, in Robert Frost's words, is what disappears in translation. A prose translation of a poem can offer little poetry, but the reader can rely on the accuracy of the "content matter" thus rendered and he need not fear, as in a poetic translation, that the imagery may be distorted and phrases left out or added for the sake of obtaining a rhyme or a rhythmic pattern.

Paraphrasing a poem in prose has been compared to playing a symphony on a single oboe. Yet this is preferable to an attempt at transferring a poem, undisturbed, from one medium to another, or, in terms of the comparison, to re-orchestrate the symphony with instruments unknown to the composer.

Contents

Chronology

1802 Nikolaus Franz Niembsch (Lenau) born on August 13 in Csatád near Temesvár (now Timisoara) in Austro-Hungary (now Rumania), as the third child (and only son) of Franz Niembsch and Therese, née Maygraber.
1803 The family moves to Pesth (Budapest).
1807 Franz Niembsch, Lenau's father, dies on April 23.
1811 Therese Niembsch, Lenau's mother, marries Dr. Karl Vogel on September 23.
1812-1815 Lenau attends a clerical *Gymnasium* (Gymnasium Pesthiensi Scholarum Piarum) in Pesth.
1816 The family moves to Tokaj in eastern Hungary. Lenau attends the *Gymnasium* in Sátoralja-Ujhely.
1817 Lenau's mother, with her five children, moves back to Pesth.
1818 Lenau completes his secondary education in Pesth.
1818-1821 Studies philosophy at the University of Vienna. During recesses, he lives with his paternal grandparents in Stockerau near Vienna.
1821 Lenau's grandfather is granted the predicate "Edler von Strehlenau."
1821-1822 Lenau studies Hungarian Law at the University of Pressburg (Bratislava).
1822-1823 Studies Agriculture in Ungarisch-Altenburg (Moson-magyaróvár).
1823-1827 Relationship with Berta Hauer.
1823-1824 Studies Philosophy at the University of Vienna.
1824-1826 Studies Austrian Law at the same university.
1826-1830 Studies Medicine at the same university.
1828 Publishes his first two poems: "Die Jugendträume," in *Aurora: Taschenbuch auf das Jahr 1828,* and "Reiterlied," in *Illyrisches Blatt,* November 29.
1829 Lenau's mother dies.
1830 Lenau's grandmother dies, leaving him a sizable sum of money.
1831 Lenau travels to Germany. Establishes contacts with the circle of "Swabian Poets"—Gustav Schwab, Ludwig Uhland, Gustav Pfizer, Justinus Kerner, Karl Mayer, and Alexander von Württemberg. Continues his medical studies (without finishing) at the University of Heidelberg. Acquaintance with Lotte Gmelin.
1832 Voyage to America. Lands in Baltimore on October 8. Travels to Pittsburgh; Economy, Pa.; Crawford County, Ohio; Niagara

Falls; and New York City. Publication of Lenau's first volume of verse, *Gedichte,* by Cotta in Stuttgart. (New editions in 1834, 1837, 1840, 1841, 1843, 1844.)

1833 Return from America. Lands in Bremen, in June.

1833-1844 Lenau lives mostly in Vienna. Regularly frequents the "Silbernes Kaffeehaus," foremost literary café in Vienna. Occasional contact with Franz Grillparzer, Anastasius Grün, Ernst von Feuchtersleben, and other poets and writers. Spends many summers in Bad Ischl, Upper Austria, and other resorts in the vicinity. Annual trips to Stuttgart. Continued friendship with the Swabian Poets.

1834 Meets Sophie Löwenthal.

1836 Publication of *Faust.* (New edition in 1840)

1837 Publication of *Savonarola.* (New, unaltered edition in 1844)

1838 Publication of *Neuere Gedichte.* (New editions in 1840, 1841, 1843, 1844.)

1839 Engagement with Karoline Unger.

1840 Engagement broken.

1842 Publication of *Die Albigenser.*

1844 Engagement with Maria Behrends in July. Total paretic collapse in October. Confined to insane asylum in Winnenthal near Stuttgart.

1847 Transferral to insane asylum in Ober-Döbling, near (now part of) Vienna, in May.

1850 Dies August 22. Buried at the Weidling cemetery.

1851 Publication of posthumous works, including *Don Juan,* edited by Anastasius Grün.

CHAPTER 1

Weltschmerz and Reality: The Poet's Life

IN the autumn of 1833, there was excitement in the literary salons and cafés of Vienna over the arrival—rather, the triumphant return—of the young poet Nikolaus Lenau, a capricious Hungarian aristocrat, a man who had traveled in America, who had the audacity, one year after Goethe's death, to write his own *Faust*, and who enjoyed being lionized by the mediocre.

To the fashion-conscious of that time, the literary vogue was *Weltschmerz*, the late Romanticists' melancholy derived from *ennui*, ironic skepticism, and a jaded irresoluteness. In the eyes of many, Lord Byron was the *Weltschmerz* poet par excellence, although his poetic genius defies reduction to so simple a formula. Alfred de Musset, Giacomo Leopardi, and Mikhail Lermontov were representatives of the movement in France, Italy, and Russia. In German literature, the works of Heinrich Heine and August von Platen show traits of it, but it was, above all, Nikolaus Lenau, "the German Byron," who was hailed as the true poet of *Weltschmerz*. Much to the detriment of his creative career, Lenau was a fashionable poet and one of the very few who were able to live comfortably on the income from their writings. Neither Goethe nor Schiller were in this position. In 1840, Lenau's publisher, Johann Georg von Cotta, told Lenau that he sold fewer than forty copies of Goethe's poems yearly.[1] Lenau, on the other hand, prided himself of the fact that young girls in Swabia took his poems along to church in place of the Bible.

Exercising little self-criticism and carried by the waves of popularity, Lenau published almost everything he wrote. His posthumous works merely fill a slim volume. It would be wrong to say that he was essentially a poet altogether different from what the Lenau cult made him out to be. His admirers met his own inclination half-way. Melancholy and despair were deeply imbedded in his psychological make-up, and the Byronic pose of *Weltschmerz* was not wholly a pose to him. Yet the grounds on which Lenau was idolized were not the same as those which show him as a great poet more than a hundred years after his death. Beneath the exterior of the facile exploiter of a literary fashion, beneath the guise of the melancholy dandy, there was a genuine, hard-working artist and an unpretentious man, gravely ill during the greatest part of his life, restless and desperate. Like Grillparzer, Lenau was alone when his creative genius was at its best. None of his devotees could understand and appreciate the true artist in him. And they would not have been willing, conversely, to accept Lenau as the plain, ordinary man he actually was.

Lenau's family background was humble.[2] He was born as Nikolaus Franz Niembsch on August 13, 1802, in Csatád, a small town near Temesvár in the "crownland" Hungary of the Austrian empire. The area, which had become part of Austria in 1718, had been colonized during the subsequent decades by German farmers and was known under the name "Hungarian Banat." In 1920 the area was divided between Rumania and Yugoslavia. The German population preserved their language and traditions until they were expelled at the end of World War II. Lenau's connection with the "Banat" is purely coincidental. His paternal grandfather and greatgrandfather had been Austrian army officers who moved about considerably. Lenau's father, Franz Niembsch, had prepared for the same career, but he married young and accepted a subaltern position in civilian government service ("Kameral-Gegenschreiber"). He happened to be stationed in Csatád when Lenau was born. Franz Niembsch showed little interest in his family, led a dissolute life, and died of consumption at the age of thirty. Lenau's mother, an impulsive, emotional woman, hailed from the German bourgeoisie of Pesth (Budapest). There was not a drop of Hungarian blood in Lenau. Although Therese Niembsch was vehemently attached to her son, she showed much less affection for her three daughters. After her husband's death, she married an unsuccessful physician and bore him two more daughters. For years, the family suffered great need and was constantly on the move. The psychological damage to the sensitive, impressionable children during these years of migration can hardly be overrated. Young Nikolaus' education, in particular, was so erratic that in 1818 his paternal grandparents insisted on having him stay with them at their home in the the town of Stockerau near Vienna. His grandfather, Colonel Joseph Niembsch, was an ambitious man. In 1821, a year before his death, upon his own application and the payment of a large fee, he was raised to the lowest rank of nobility and granted the dreamed-up predicate "Edler von Strehlenau." Hence Lenau's "aristocratic" background. Later on, the poet chose the last two syllables of the title as his pseudonym.

Despite the external security which his grandparents' home provided, Lenau's school work remained undisciplined, and he could not decide on a course of study. From 1818 to 1821 he was matriculated at the University of Vienna and took courses in Philosophy, Religion, Mathematics, Physics, and History. In 1821-1822 he studied Hungarian Law in Pressburg; next in 1822-1823 he tried his hand at the College of Agriculture in Ungarisch-Altenburg (now Mosonmagyaróvár); in 1823-1824 he took up Philosophy in Vienna, and in 1824-1826, Austrian Law and Political Science.

During these years of study, Lenau began to write poetry. One of his sisters, Therese, had married a government official by the name of Anton Xaver Schurz, an occasional and less than mediocre poet and admirer of pre-Goethean lyric poetry. Under Schurz' tutelage, Lenau wrote imitative odes in the tradition of Klopstock and Hölty. During these formative years, he had his deepest and most genuine love experience. The facts concerning his relationship with Berta Hauer are largely unknown. Berta, apparently a vivacious child of the lower classes, was a very attractive fifteen-year-old when Lenau met her in 1823. There can be little doubt that he was the father of a child born to her in 1826. According to his letters to friends, he was extremely happy with Berta and planned to marry her. Yet, for reasons unknown, he broke off the relationship in 1827. Biographers put the blame on Berta and have made her out to be an adventuress and worse,[3] despite the fact that there is no reason, from what little we know, to question her character and her loyalty. It is possible that Lenau's aristocratic grandmother, hearing of his marriage plans, had threatened to cut off the funds that supported Lenau; it could also be that Lenau's own feelings for Berta had cooled or that the two had an irreparable rift. Lenau's desperate reaction to the break could lead one to conclude that the initiative had come from Berta, but this was not the case. The unhappy experience left a deep scar on Lenau, and there is evidence in his letters that he suffered from the loss of Berta for many years and that he never ceased thinking of her. In his poetry after this break, despair and transiency emerged as the predominant themes. It would be wrong, however, to assume a relationship of cause and effect. Lenau's melancholic disposition was innate. The unfortunate end of the love affair merely reaffirmed a tendency which he characterized as a "gravitation toward misfortune" (III, 154).[4] Significantly, too, Lenau's love for Berta inspired hardly any love poems. The few he wrote are mere exercises in classical forms. But the unhappy end of the relationship brought on a great number of the poetic lamentations and induced Lenau to discover his own tone and style.

When Lenau's grandmother died in 1830, he inherited a considerable sum of money and set out on a journey. He planned to go to Heidelberg and continue his medical studies there; but this was not the primary reason for going to Germany. Lenau had decided, by that time, that writing poetry would be his true vocation, and he was eager to establish literary contacts in Germany and publish his poems there. This was a widely accepted custom among those Austrian writers who refused to submit their works to the bureau of censorship. Conditions in Germany at the time were more auspicious for poets and writers. It was suggested to Lenau that he approach the publisher Cotta and get to know the circle of poets residing in and about Stuttgart, the "Swabian Poets," whose recommendations carried weight with Cotta. Full of enthusiasm, he set out in the summer of 1831.[5]

In Stuttgart he was received most cordially by the local poets who immediately recognized in him a talent superior to their own. They were friends to Lenau's liking. Morbidly sensitive to criticism, he never sought the company of his true peers but liked to associate with minor literary figures. The Swabian Poets were essentially late Romanticists with a strong religious bent. They turned out moralizing nature poetry, pleasant vignettes of moderate artistic value. They are best described as kind men, family-centered, uncomplicated and unexcitable, and endowed with considerably more intelligence and wisdom than most literary historians acknowledge. There was Gustav Schwab, a trained theologian and teacher at a Stuttgart secondary school, and a man well versed in the historical foundations of Mysticism and Pietism. He was one of the exponents of a newly awakened movement of religious orthodoxy that had its center in Württemberg. In nearby Weinsberg, Lenau became acquainted with Justinus Kerner, author of *Die Seherin von Prevorst* (The Visionary of Prevorst), a physician, occultist, and charming eccentric endowed with a fertile imagination. Gustav Pfizer, another theologian-turned-poet, also belonged to the group, as did Karl Mayer, a judge in Waiblingen near Stuttgart, and Count Alexander von Württemberg. The only true poet of the circle was Ludwig Uhland in Tübingen. Considerably reserved and outwardly pedantic, he was never as close to Lenau as the others.

The dark, enigmatic nobleman from Hungary, surrounded by an aura of demonic discontent, fascinated the Swabians and their wives and daughters. Immediately they set out to cure Lenau's melancholy by trying to show him the way back to religious belief, which he had lost in his student days, and to put an end to his bachelorhood. At first they seemed to make headway in both directions. Lenau, although not genuinely religious, had a lifelong interest in theological questions and was an eager partner in discussions on the subject. And he had met, soon after his arrival in Stuttgart, Schwab's niece, the musically gifted but otherwise undistinguished Lotte Gmelin. Lenau was immediately drawn to the nineteen-year-old girl, and the Schwabs were delighted. Yet Lenau, from the very beginning, had made up his mind that he was not the right match for Lotte. "I shall renounce this girl" (III, 88), he wrote to Schurz in November, 1831. In two other letters he expressed the reason for his renunciation through an image: He did not have the courage, he wrote, to "attach this heavenly rose" to his "gloomy (*nächtliches*) heart" (III, 92, 138). It is impossible to tell how attached Lenau actually was to Lotte and whether his attitude was not merely a polite, if excessively dramatic, way of bowing out. It is unlikely that Lenau would have been eager, at that time, to settle down to a family life.

After a few weeks in Stuttgart, Lenau traveled to Heidelberg, there to pursue his medical studies. His initial enthusiasm was great, but soon he was spending most of his time over Spinoza's *Ethics*. The pantheistic idea that all substance is of God and will eventually revert to Him, left a deep impression on Lenau. He alludes to this idea in his letters, and it recurs in several later poems. The study of Spinoza gave him hours of serenity in what proved to be depressing months in the small university town. Heidelberg's gaiety left no trace in Lenau's letters. A deep, morbid melancholy progressively clouded his mind. He yearned for death, felt as though his soul's tendons had been cut, and was as oppressed, he wrote, as if he were carrying a corpse with him (III, 97). The intensity of his depression transcended the pose of *Weltschmerz,* for it had the marks of a pathological affliction. One can be almost certain that Lenau was, in fact, gravely ill at that time. The exact date of his syphilitic infection cannot be determined, but it is very likely that he had contracted the disease, which was then incurable and frequently a cause for suicide, in the fall of 1831. Contemporary medicine was not aware of a direct connection between syphilis and dementia paralytica, which then could be neither recognized nor treated. In subsequent years, Lenau apparently gained the impression that he had been cured; his later marriage plans would so indicate. But his natural tendency toward despair was augmented, for the rest of his life, by the physical affliction that beset him.

When Lenau's restlessness became more acute, he abandoned his studies. He traveled aimlessly between Heidelberg, Stuttgart, Tübingen, Weinsberg, and Waiblingen, visiting his friends. Early in 1932 he began to harbor a project that horrified those sedentary folk: he wanted to travel to America.[6] He considered such a journey a radical cure for his melancholy and hoped that it would inspire him with new poetic ideas. To Mayer he wrote:

> I want to send my imagination to school—to the forest primeval. I want to purge my heart in pain, in yearning for those I love. Perfection as an artist is my prime purpose in life, and I consider the strength of my mind and the happiness of my soul only means to that end. (III, 142).

Actually, Lenau's plan was not so very extraordinary. Ever since early Romanticism, a connection was seen between artistic creativity and travel.

It was the English who had discovered the joys of traveling. Jonathan Swift and Daniel Defoe had used the travel motif with varying symbolic connotations. Lawrence Sterne's *A Sentimental Journey through France and Italy* (1768) was one of the first works particularly concerned with the connection between travel and artistic inspiration. The novel had a great vogue in Germany. Goethe's travel books had become models of the genre in German Literature and influenced Friedrich Matthisson, Wilhelm Wackenroder, Ludwig Tieck, and Wilhelm Müller to describe their trips through Italy, Switzerland, and Germany. Heine's *Reisebilder* appeared from 1826 to 1831. Most important, however, as an influence on Lenau, was Lord Byron's *Childe Harold's Pilgrimage* (1812).

America as a destination was no longer a novelty either. Such dissimilar personalities as François René de Chateaubriand, Adelbert von Chamisso, and Alexander von Humboldt had traversed and described that country. In England, Samuel Taylor Coleridge and Robert Southey had planned to emigrate to America in 1794, with the intention of establishing a "pantisocratic" community free from prejudice and tradition. Emigration societies abounded on the continent, especially after the unsuccessful revolution of 1830 when many sought political refuge overseas. The Romantic generation considered America a land of Utopia, a paradise of freedom, and a realm of unimagined scenic beauty.

Lenau's plans to go to America were haphazard and vague, to be sure, and his reasons changed from one day to the next. He averred that he wanted to buy land and improve his financial status, which had suffered when he lost about half of his small fortune in an unlucky speculation in a Viennese bank. He fancied that he might complete his medical studies and become a physician in America; he gave thought, too, to lecturing on aesthetics at an American university; at other times, the life of a settler in the West appeared more attractive to him. In planning the duration of his stay, Lenau vacillated between plans for five years (III, 141) and three weeks (III, 185), and he even wished he were back from America before he had left (III, 169).

Lenau's friends and relatives tried everything to dissuade him from the vague enterprise. Kerner even wrote a letter to the chairman of an emigration society which Lenau had contacted, telling him that Mr. von Niembsch was a mental patient who had escaped from his institution with the *idée fixe* that he was an ape and should seek his abode in the vast American forests primeval. All arrangements, therefore, made by the patient should be cancelled immediately. But it seems that Dr. Kerner's letter had come too late.

Lenau sailed from Amsterdam in July, 1832, and landed in Chesapeake Bay after a hazardous ten-week voyage in an ancient Dutch vessel. He quickly passed through Baltimore, bought a horse and traveled across Pennsylvania, stopping at Bedford and Pittsburgh, and visiting the colony of the Harmonists in Economy, the most successful of the numerous religious "communistic" settlements of that time.[7] Founded by Johann Georg Rapp in 1805, they were called the "Rappists." The colony was extremely prosperous at the time and constituted a great attraction for many

European visitors. Several wool and silk factories flourished there, but Lenau was especially impressed by the intense religious life of the community.

From Pennsylvania he proceeded to Ohio. There Lenau bought four hundred acres of land for $500 in Crawford County, near the present town of Bucyrus. Lenau traveled with many pieces of luggage, including his violin. Subsequently, he returned to Economy and spent several months there, but at Christmas he returned to his farmland, lived at a neighbor's house, and made a few half-hearted attempts to begin the clearing of his property. Neighbors remembered him as a refined gentleman, elegantly dressed in a fur coat, dancing pumps, and white gloves. At times, he would deal a few axe blows at a tree here and there, then give up quickly. He allegedly was referred to as "the crazy German."[8]

Once again, Lenau left for Pittsburgh and Economy. During his long winter journeys, he had become afflicted with rheumatism and had to be nursed back to health. In March he leased his farm land in Ohio to a German carpenter who was expected to clear the property. Then he made his long-planned trip to Niagara Falls, the one place he had specifically yearned to see. Continuing along the newly opened Erie Canal to Albany, and from there down the Hudson River, he reached New York in the middle of April, 1833. Late in April or early in May, Lenau sailed from New York to Bremen. He had been in America for about seven months.

During his entire journey, Lenau was greatly hampered linguistically; he had what would now be called a "limited reading knowledge" of English, so that his only contacts were fellow Germans, except for one lawyer in Bedford, Pa., with whom he could converse in Latin. The only time Lenau made an impression on his American hosts was when he played the violin at a soirée in the home of a justice of the peace (a former Prussian officer) in Pittsburgh. As a student in Vienna, he had had excellent training on the instrument. Until that evening, his listeners agreed, such playing had not been heard west of the Alleghenies. The letters Lenau wrote from America show that he had been lonely, unhappy, and easily annoyed during the entire sojourn. He made no effort to understand the country and its people on their own terms. What inspired most European visitors—the political atmosphere in the New World—left him cold. His basic outlook was aristocratic, and, despite occasional diatribes against tyrants, the very idea of democracy disgusted him.

The financial gain to Lenau from his time in America was nil. He failed to pay taxes on his property, and the investment would have been a complete loss had not a new owner, of his own good will, returned the original sum to Lenau's relations. The poetic gain was considerable, although not as great as Lenau had hoped. About a dozen poems deal directly with motifs pertaining to the journey—the sea, Indians, Niagara Falls—and a few others show a more tenuous influence. Part of his first long lyric-epic poem *Faust* reflects experiences gained on the trip.

The American experience proved to be, least of all, the hoped-for panacea for Lenau's permanent state of depression. If anything, he had been confirmed, by his subjective outlook, in his belief that man can draw no consolation from the world in which he has to live. All in all, Lenau's trip to America, although not strictly a disaster, may be called a disappointment on most counts, and the reason for this should not be sought in America.

Upon Lenau's return, Kerner provided a gesture of comic relief. When Lenau did not arrive in Stuttgart as quickly as his friends had expected, Kerner sent word to them that Lenau had come finally, but that he was in such bad shape that he had to stay at Kerner's for the time being. Not only was Lenau completely penniless, Kerner wrote, without a shirt, in rags, covered with dust, filth, and a pernicious, ominously sounding disease called "Schiffsraude" (seafarers' mange), but he was also badly mutilated: an amorous she-ape of the American forests had, out of sheer passion, bitten off Lenau's nose "down to the root."[9] Kerner was embarrassed when he received many packages with clothing, laundry, money, and consoling letters for Lenau, and the senders were in a huff when they realized that they had missed the joke.

When Lenau did arrive in Stuttgart, in July, 1833, he found himself established as a well-known poet. His first book of poems, *Gedichte* (1832), had appeared while he was in America, and had been enthusiastically received. Lenau now felt certain that he had found his true vocation. More than ever he was determined to give his all to art, to "crucify himself if this should result in a good poem" (III, 142). He had good reason, years later, to say that his works were his life, since he had found no room for deeds (IV, 392).

Thenceforth, new and ever augmented editions of his poems

regularly appeared on the market. The volume *Gedichte* was reissued in seven editions between 1832 and 1844. In 1838, Lenau brought out an altogether new collection, *Neuere Gedichte,* which was to see four more editions in subsequent years. Each of these collections was arranged in "books," and each book in groups under titles, such as *Sehnsucht, Erinnerung, Phantasien, Heidebilder, Polenlieder, Atlantica, Liebesklänge.* In 1851, Lenau's Austrian fellow poet, Anastasius Grün, edited a collection of posthumous poems. Altogether, Lenau wrote some 370 poems, including such occasional verse as dedications and entries in friends' diaries. His opus also comprises four long poems containing lyric, epic, and dramatic elements: *Faust, Savonarola, Die Albigenser,* and *Don Juan;* a small fragment of a drama, *Helena;* some 880 published letters; and one book review.

Lenau spent the remaining eleven years of his sane life mostly in Vienna, but he traveled to Stuttgart at least once every year. Although his friendship with the Swabian Poets continued, it cooled somewhat, mostly because of Lenau's hypersensitivity to their well-meant advice and criticism. When in Stuttgart, he made his home with a couple by the name of Reinbeck. Georg Reinbeck was a secondary school teacher, a fastidious and dry Prussian who had a difficult time among the earthy Swabian youths; his wife Emilie liked to paint. With great patience, they provided Lenau with the external comforts that were so important to him, but they were no match for him intellectually or artistically. When in Vienna, Lenau lived at the house of Schurz or with a family he had come to know after his return from America. In 1834 at the "Silbernes Kaffeehaus"—a locality much frequented by poets and writers—he had met Max Löwenthal, a wealthy government official and occasional poet, who introduced him to his home and his twenty-four-year-old wife Sophie. A striking beauty, Sophie was referred to as "the irresistible one" in Viennese society and she was accustomed to being the hub of attention. Lenau's admiration for her quickly turned into an affection which Sophie returned. For the rest of his days, the great agony and the few joys that his love for Sophie brought him were the dominant feature in Lenau's existence. Sophie was, with regard to Lenau's private life, the worst possible partner imaginable. Sentimental, overbearing, and calculating, she was too intelligent to be shrugged off as a flirtatious socialite, too substantial to be dismissed as a permanent adolescent. The complexity of their relationship is unfathomable. There is no end to the psychological strata that could be uncovered. Did Lenau really love her, or did he feel a need for the pain their unfulfilled relationship caused him? Were Sophie's desperate pleas that they curb their passion genuine, or was there nothing to curb, and the two merely relished the roles of the troubadour and the unattainable lady? Sophie's marriage was repulsive to her; she withdrew from Max after their third and last child was born. She exacted an oath from Lenau that he would seek no physical relationship with other women, and Lenau seems to have kept his oath. In vain she tried to elicit the same promise from her husband. A psychologically inclined critic has suggested, with good reason, that Sophie was neurotic and frigid.[10] Lenau made frequent and unsuccessful attempts to break away from her. His trips to Stuttgart were, in part, flights from Sophie, followed by returns to her.

Sophie influenced Lenau strongly in his attitude toward religion. He was a member of the late-Romantic generation that considered religious belief an intellectual issue, in contrast to the earlier Romanticists who had embraced religion on more emotional terms. In their fascination with the subconscious, the archetypal and the spiritual, and with the hereafter as a fulfillment of life, the early Romanticists had introduced supernatural religion into poetic thought. Belief in the hereafter was, to them, a device to enhance poetic creativity. Religion began to have a function and to serve a purpose, instead of existing a priori. This trend became even more apparent in Lenau's generation. Many of those who espoused religion did so because belief in God provided them with a metaphysical shelter. They considered it a therapeutic medium, a panacea for their torn souls. The reawakening of religious orthodoxy and mysticism, to which Lenau was exposed among the Swabian Poets, can be viewed from this angle.

Lenau's relationship with Sophie confirmed his need for religious bonds. An intensely devout woman, Sophie encouraged him to see their love as part of a religious experience and to substitute the love of God for their own unfulfilled desires. Lenau accepted the challenge and began to glorify Sophie as a pseudo-deity. Between April, 1836, and August, 1843, he sent or gave her over three hundred love notes, short letters he wrote when he was away from her. Some critics have made exaggerated claims about the literary quality of these notes.[11]

Their foremost significance is that of biographical documents. They are steeped in religious thoughts and imagery and bespeak not only Lenau's eagerness to please Sophie, who relished the mystic-sensuous impact of his messages, but also the poet's attempt to find a new attitude toward himself and to seek refuge under a safe shelter: "I cannot think of God without thinking of you" (IV, 21); "When I love you, I am near God, for He is in you" (IV, 46). He called her the "favorite creation of a personal, loving God" (IV, 45) and imagined holding her close to himself "at the feet of God" (IV, 134). The parallels between love for Sophie and love for God are pursued at length and, at times, in frenzied images. The bulk of the love notes dates from 1836 and 1837, the years when Lenau wrote *Savonarola,* his one major attempt to give poetic expression to his newly found religiosity. The tone and imagery of this poem is reminiscent of the diction of the love notes.

Lenau's high-pitched mysticism proved to be a quickly passing phase. In retrospect, it appeared artificial to him. He regretted having written *Savonarola,* and his last two long poems, *Die Albigenser* and *Don Juan,* follow altogether different paths. His attempts to find peace by submitting himself to a firm belief in a divine order had failed and were abandoned. Subsequently, he turned against Mysticism and cast aside what he had glorified. Concurrently, his love notes to Sophie became fewer and eventually petered out. In later years they lost their mystic imagery and were little more than records of tormented introspection.

Although Lenau had relinquished the religious basis for his love to Sophie, he could not or would not break with her. Their relationship became increasingly painful, and Sophie's skill at keeping her lover at a distance without discouraging him was strained to the utmost. Twice, Lenau came close to getting married. In 1839 he was introduced to Karoline Unger, one of the great singers of the period and a one-time protégée of Beethoven's. The two artists came to like each other, and finally Lenau had to break the news to Sophie that they were planning to be married. "It is up to you," he wrote to her, "to exercise human kindness toward my torn heart" (IV, 331). Sophie reacted in predictable fashion. She answered by informing Lenau that her health was failing and that she felt her end approaching. (She outlived Lenau by forty years.) Then she arranged for a meeting with him, told him derogatory rumors about Karoline, and persuaded him to break with the singer. Lenau lent her a willing ear and finally broke off the engagement.

From 1840 on, Lenau's health began to fail. He suffered from nervous disorders, chronic fatigue and sleeplessness, symptoms that were, in his case, indicative of the approaching paretic collapse. Merely forty, he had the appearance of an old man. Yet he was driven by an enervating restlessness. In 1840 he made three laborious trips to Stuttgart and back, and in the winter of 1841-1842 he changed apartments three times. Under constant physical and mental tribulation, he wrote his most ambitious lyric cycle, "Waldlieder," and his dramatic poem *Don Juan,* a product of febrile erotic phantasies springing from an awareness of a consuming physical debility.

The circumstances of Lenau's next and final marriage project show that he was no longer in full control of his mental powers. In June, 1844, ailing and depressed, he went to the spa of Baden-Baden, partly to restore his health, partly to submerge himself in an atmosphere of frivolity provided by the fashionable international clientele of the famous watering place. He felt that this environment would be conducive to the progress of his *Don Juan.* His health did not improve and he had premonitions of his approaching end. "I am sinking ever faster and falling precipitously" (*Es geht mit beschleunigter Geschwindigkeit holpernd und stürzend talab* [V, 197]), he wrote to Sophie. A change in his personality became apparent. He insulted such old friends as the Reinbecks and opened his heart to people he had never liked, such as the writer Bertold Auerbach. In Baden-Baden, Lenau met a lady from Frankfurt am Main and her niece, the thirty-two year old Maria Behrends, the daughter of a late mayor of Frankfurt. A few days later, he proposed to her, much to the consternation of her relatives who did not know what to make of the situation and hardly dared to hope that the famous poet's intentions were serious. Maria was a quiet, unassuming person. The calming effect her company had on the unnerved, ill poet was enough to make him woo her. He traveled to Frankfurt twice, and the engagement was announced early in August. Lenau fluctuated between paroxysms of frenzied happiness, in which he imagined himself in scenes of marital bliss, and attacks of despondency. For the time being, he withheld the news of his engagement from Sophie, but she read about it in the papers. Later in August, Lenau went to Vienna, saw Sophie, and listened to her disquieting if justified words of warning against entering into a liaison haphazardly. His despondency grew, and his physical condition worsened.

In September, while at the Reinbeck's in Stuttgart, he suffered a slight paralytic stroke, accompanied by an impairment of speech. He seemed to recover at first, but had grave doubts about his marriage plans. A strong wish for peace and quiet dominated his thinking. In faltering syntax he wrote to Sophie: "Most of all, I would like to die, but I want it so weary and weak as if one wants to lie down when one is very weary (*Ich möchte am liebsten sterben, doch wünsch ich mirs jetzt so müd und schwach, wie man sich gern niederlegt, wenn man recht müd ist* [V, 233f.]. During the following weeks, his thoughts became increasingly incoherent, and his actions showed him to be less and less in touch with reality. At times he mastered his thinking and became aware of his mental aberrations. Repeatedly, he expressed horror at the thought of becoming insane. Not knowing the medical reason for his incipient breakdown, he saw himself as the victim of his own mental and nervous excesses—an explanation that does have some marginal validity. In Lenau's own eyes he had fulfilled the promise that he would crucify himself if this act would result in a good poem. He had given everything to art. In these excruciating weeks of waning mental coherence, he said to a son of his recently deceased friend Count Alexander von Württemberg that there is a region in man's nerves that ought to remain untouched and sacred, a depth where absolute peace must prevail. But in his case, he explained, these depths had been agitated, and for this he had to pay.[12] When his condition deteriorated further and he became physically violent, the Reinbecks were forced to have him taken to an insane asylum in Winnenthal near Stuttgart.[13] In 1847 he was transferred to a similar institution in Ober-Döbling near Vienna. His case of *dementia paralytica* progressed typically. He died on August 22, 1850, after he had been reduced to a purely vegetative form of existence in his last years.

Lenau's life was ill-starred, sad, and inconsequential. Unlike Byron, he was not fortunate enough to lead a life on which part of his fame could rest. There was great truth in his statement to Sophie that his life consisted only of his poems.

CHAPTER 2

Topoi *and Experiences: The Emerging Artist*

I *Fruitful Imitation*

THE beginnings of a poet's own language and style, of his own tone unmistakable from the imitative patterns of his early literary exercises, is one of the great miracles in literary art. In German literature, Goethe and Rilke are often cited as poets whose incipient creative independence is both readily discernible and of great influence on one or several generations of poets. Goethe, trained in the artificial idiom of Anacreontic poetry, created the direct, forceful language of what came to be known as his "Storm and Stress" period. His language became the model for the literature of a century. Following the traditions of literary Impressionism, Rilke's early poetic exercises painted little mood pictures, simple and pleasant, but of no lasting value; he turned into a poet when he coined his own symbolic idiom that helped him to express a subtler reality behind appearances.

Lenau's literary apprenticeship and his discovery of his own poetic impulses can be traced as closely as that of Goethe and Rilke. His beginnings were strangely antiquated and out of touch with the time in which he lived. A young man with poetic aspirations, growing up in the 1820s, could well be expected to have come into contact with the Classic-Romantic tradition in German letters, to have come to terms with the works of Goethe, Schiller, Novalis, and Tieck. He might have become acquainted with intellectual movements and phenomena of the preceding decades: the literary revolution of the Storm and Stress; German Idealism; the spell exercised by folk songs and fairy tales over highly sophisticated intellectuals; the fascination of the Weimar group with Greece; their concept of "Humanität," triumphing over all dark, hostile forces; Romantic Irrationalism; the Romanticists' probing of the unconscious and their interest in everything remote in time and space.

Although all these ideas were in the forefront of contemporary literary thought, they did not affect Lenau. He formed his poetic style on altogether different models: Friedrich Klopstock and the so-called "Göttinger Hainbund," a group of poets of the bucolic, pastoral tradition. Klopstock (1724-1803) was the first German poet of the eighteenth century to free himself from the limitations of Rationalism and to substitute enthusiasm and emotion for cerebral brilliance. An adherent of Pietism, he reintroduced religious thought into poetry. Among the members of the *Hainbund,* which flourished in the 1770s, Ludwig Hölty (1748-1776) was the most important influence on Lenau. His poetry, by far inferior to that of Klopstock, depicted stereotype nature settings characterized by rose-colored sunsets, pink clouds, shady groves, and picturesque shepherds. In the forms of the classical ode, Hölty sang to the joys of love and friendship, of sorrow and death. His carefully guarded restriction to stereotype views kept him from reality, away from the desire to look at the world perceptively and with an eye for details.

Lenau chose the *Hainbund* poets as his literary mentors under the guidance of Schurz, his brother-in-law and his senior by eight years. Schurz admitted that he was not familiar with "more recent" literature.[1] Lenau's first poems were written in the style of the *Hainbund* poetry. His imitative verses, begun in 1821 and extending to about 1827, are skillful and show a fine mastery of literary forms, but they could have been written by almost any talented young writer. His preferred forms were classical stanzas, such as had been in great vogue in eighteenth-century Germany. He wrote a variety of odes, elegies, and ghasels, sometimes jotting down the meter above the poem. The themes of his early poems were traditional, too. There are apostrophes, reminiscences, lamentations, and stylized nature hymns. He expropriated from his models, especially Hölty, not only themes and situations, but also the vocabulary and certain rhetorical phrases, such as "kisses of fire," "blissful hour," "spring's radiant glance," or such metonymies as "friend of quiet contemplation (standing for "night")" or "the cheek's blossoms of delight (for "tears of joy")." He liked to depict scenes of undisturbed bliss, as for instance in his "Abendbild," following Horace's version of the Sapphic strophe:

Schon zerfließt das ferne Gebirg mit Wolken
In ein Meer; den Wogen entsteigt der Mond, er

Grüßt die Flur, entgegen ihm grüßt das schönste
Lied Philomelens. (I, 464)

("The distant mountains merge with clouds, forming a sea; from the waves rises the moon. It greets the pasture and is greeted by Philomela's most beautiful song.")

There are stylized love songs, addressed to Berta, and even a highly rhetorical attack upon tyrants, "An einen Tyrannen" (I, 464), an ode in the Alcaic strophe and so stereotyped that it did not attract the attention of the Austrian bureau of censorship when it appeared in Lenau's first book of poems in 1832.

Despite the imitative nature of his early attempts, Lenau's preoccupation with the literary style of a bygone age came to mean more to him than simple exercises in craftsmanship. He took seriously the rosy idealism of the *Hainbund* poets and fully embraced their artfully simplified vision of an eternal harmony in the universe. In his youthful enthusiasm he accepted as a philosophy what should at best have been an exercise book.

The first gradual change discernible in Lenau's poems is a shift in his topical interests. In the years 1826 and 1827 he wrote many poems about sickness and death, transiency and despair. In some the language is the same as that of the early poems, studded with the rhetorical devices of Lenau's literary models. It was to be expected that the ephemeral idealism in his thinking would not prevail for long. He turned toward sorrowful subject matter, but the fact that his poetic diction had not changed sufficiently to convey, always and convincingly, the despair and melancholy shows that Lenau's gravitation toward the realm of grief and sadness was not a deeply felt experience from the very beginning. He merely followed a literary fashion, and it was only gradually that Lenau came to feel deeply the experiences about which he was writing and found strong, original images to convey them.

The poem "Die Mutter am Grabe ihres Kindes" (I, 470) deals with a sorrowful subject matter in a formal, superficial idiom: "The wind blows over the grave; the mother's tears turn into ice because cruel death has wilted the lovely roses on the cheeks of her child." The poem is not simple and straightforward enough to pass as a folk song, and it does not ring true enough to convey a genuine inner experience. The same discrepancy between subject matter and diction appears in a number of poems from the period. In "Dahin" (I, 471), the past and the present are juxtaposed: "In the past, the beloved kissed the tear of joy from the poet's face, but now the roaring storm carries away the burning tear of sadness." And in "An die Hoffnung" (I, 472), the poet, in his despair, will entrust himself to hope only if she (an allegorical figure) will direct him with a consoling smile into the nocturnal realm of death. The diction in these poems is too conventional to convey any strong sentiment or carry through the themes treated.

But it happens intermittently that Lenau uses a conventional rhetorical figure in a surprising way. In the poem "Am Bette eines Kindes" (I, 89), he expresses the hope that sleep will deliver the child to its "more serious brother" death, lest the child have to face the world; for "mit gezücktem Dolche harrt der Kummer / An der seligen Kindheit Pforte meines / Lieblings" ("with a dagger drawn, grief is lurking at the gateway of my darling's blissful childhood"). This image is effective through its intensity. Sorrow would not normally be associated with so violent an image as a figure with a drawn dagger. The association stands out in the poem and rings poetically true.

In another poem of the same period, "Die Felsenplatte" (I, 33), Lenau rendered very conventionally the thoughts and sensations of a young man. While leaning against a rock, he reminisces about the loss of all things dear to him. In the last stanza, a storm comes up, and the poem ends with a flash of lightning illuminating the rock. It is a surprising ending, not altogether in key with the rest of the purely rhetorical lines:

> Zu den Füßen des Vertieften,
> Zuckt der Stein jetzt bleich und kahl.

("At the feet of the youth lost in thought, the stone now flickers, pale and barren.")

The last line is the only memorable one in the poem. The flash of lightning is transferred from the sky to the stone; the stone is "bleich" (pale), an adjective normally associated in German with people, not with objects. Thus Lenau established a symbolic connection between the inanimate stone and the young man—an unexpected turn in an otherwise undistinguished literary exercise.

It was the idea of transiency in particular that Lenau dwelt on in his early poems and for which he first found, then created, a great variety of verbal images. In an ode in the Sapphic meter, written in 1822 or 1823, "An der Bahre der Geliebten" (I, 89), he associated the fleeting waves of a brook with his beloved's premonitions of death: "She turned her face toward the fleeting waves, as if she heard the whisper of the dark voices of the future." Here future represents death, for the girl is now lying on her bier. The transiency of life and the inevitability of death are conveyed through the image of running water. The same device was used in "Das Rosenmädchen" (I, 462), written one or two years later. A maiden tends roses, for her own pleasure, in the midst of a grove. After her roses have wilted and her nightingales have ceased to sing, she stands by a waterfall and reflects on transiency. In terms of imagery, the dependence of these poems on the verse of Klopstock and the *Hainbund* poets is evident. "Das Rosenmädchen," in particular, can be traced back to Hölty's "Der Anger," "Mailied," and "Seufzer," and to Klopstock's "Der Bach."[2] Yet Lenau introduced one characteristic innovation. Whereas waterfalls and brooks, as part of the stylized landscape of the *Hainbund* poets, are associated with an aura of peace and bliss, Lenau connected the murmuring waterfall with the motif of transiency. This is, in fact, the only characteristic by which a poem such as "Das Rosenmädchen" can be distinguished from *Hainbund* poetry. Lenau found an image in his models and used it in a novel context.

Lenau proceeded differently in one of his more ambitious early poems, "Die Zweifler" (I, 55). It may be considered his desperate *credo* of the inconsistency that prevails in the world, in each individual, and in the universe. Two youths enter a grove adorned with blossoms. The sun is setting, and a nightingale calls from the bushes. But this realm of bliss does not last. It is created only to be destroyed:

In seinem Durste wird der Tod
Hinweg dein süßes Lied auch trinken,
Du wirst vom stillen Aste sinken!

("Death, in his thirst, will drink away your sweet song, and you will fall off the silent branch.")

The flowers that listen, like the children, to a wanderer's fairy tales, are admonished not to believe them. A storm is drawing near, and soon they will be torn from their green bed by the furiously roaring river. One of the youths sums up these images:

Vergänglichkeit! Wie rauschen deine Wellen
Dahin durchs Lebenslabyrinth so laut!
In deine Wirbel flüchten alle Quellen,

Kein Damm, kein Schutz sich dir entgegenbaut!
(I, 56)

("Transiency! How loudly your waves rush through the labyrinth of life. All springs flee into your whirlpools, and no dam, no shield can be set up against you.")

The river widens, the poem continues, and yet there are fools standing at its bank, lost in their dreams of immortality. Lenau reemphasized the water image by referring it to man: Deep within each individual runs the same stream.

Es braust in meines Herzens wildem Takt,
Vergänglichkeit, dein lauter Katarakt!

("In the wild beat of my heart, oh transiency, roars your loud cataract.")

There is no escape from the pattern of a pervading cataclysm. A searching glance toward the stars reveals only their evanescence. They grow pale as they see the spreading horrid sea and anticipate the day when they, now a radiant host, will fall like a tired flight of swallows.

Dann brütet auf dem Ozean die Nacht,
Dann ist des Todes großes Werk vollbracht;
Dann stockt und starrt zu Eis die grause Flut,
Worin der Wunsch des finstern Gottes ruht.
(I, 57)

("Then night will brood upon the ocean; then death has accomplished his great work; then the frightful deluge turns torpid and is congealed into ice, as the sinister god desired it.")

The sinister god is death. His satisfied smile at a universe covered with a congealed flood is the only gleam of light above the eternal ice. The starting point of this scene was a traditional rhetorical topos, "Todesflut"—the flood of death. Death and water have always been associated, in literature as well as in the archetypal experiences of mankind. The original metaphor of the flood of death must have been created by a poet as a result of profound and genuine experience. Through the ages it became well-worn, was used unthinkingly, and gradually turned into a cliché. A poet may, after a profound search for a verbal equivalent to a deeply felt sensation, arrive at such a figure of speech—"heartache" and "mad with love" can be cited as additional examples—and then realize that it is "old," and that he may have been guilty of using it many times before as a thoughtless rhetorical phrase. Similarly, Lenau used the metaphor "flood of death" many times early in his poetic career as part of the poetic idiom he had acquired as an apprentice.

> Meines Herzens matten Schlägen
> Rauscht die Todesflut entgegen.

(The feeble beats of my heart are met by the flood of death)

These lines he had written in the poem, "In der Krankheit" (I, 116), but even there the term was part of an image that does show considerable originality: Lenau wrote the poem during an illness, and captured in effective images the irresistible movement of his life toward a terminal point where death is waiting.

In "Die Zweifler," Lenau reexperienced and recreated the image of the flood of death, but he spun out the metaphor, extended it, and turned it into a haunting scene. Transiency, seen as an uncontrolled river, ravishing the universe, then turning into a stagnant ocean and eventually into ice, has become a true experience to the poet as well as to the reader. The image is no longer a purely rhetorical device used to illustrate an idea; it has moved into the foreground and affects the reader directly. He need not refer the image to an underlying abstract concept in order to comprehend it. It has attained independence and has ceased to be an intellectually contrived correlative.

Lenau became a poet when he had learned to convey, in his own idiom, truth as he experienced it; and, for Lenau, truth became more and more limited to the dismal aspects of life. The image of falling and rushing water became one of his favorites to convey his inner experiences. He used it in many variations, and with great virtuosity. In the poem "Das Mondlicht" (I, 11), young Lenau psychologically deepened the water-transiency motif. He depicted a nocturnal river scene, with the flowing water illuminated by the newly-risen moon. On the moonlit stretches, the water can be clearly seen rushing downwards irresistibly. When it runs in the shadow, it seems to be standing still, but the ear catches the sound of its unceasing motion. In the last three stanzas, the poet compares the glance of his beloved to the light of the moon, and various moments of his life to the moonlit and dark stretches of water: Whenever he awaits her in vain at night, the stream of life seems sadly to stand still; but when her light shines over its waves, he sees them rush away all too fast. In an earlier stanza, Lenau had stated that the moontrack offered a bridge across his agitated life to a grove of peace beyond, associating the moonlit water with the theme of transiency and death in general. Thus love, it seems, serves only to illuminate the downward rush of the poet's doomed life. The poem is subtle in tone and construction, and connects skillfully accurate observation of nature with deep emotions.

The image of rushing water never lost its appeal for Lenau. In his last poem, "Blick in den Strom" (I, 537), written in September, 1844, a few days before the onset of his insanity, he again connected the image of a river psychologically with man's emotions. While the poet contemplates a river—the very image of life "where everything moves and vanishes"—his soul achieves an equanimity that verges on oblivion. In a letter to Sophie, written a few days before he composed the poem, Lenau stated its motif: "Whenever one is separated from something very dear and mourns the loss, it is good to look into a river, where everything moves and vanishes like the best things in life. My melancholy would have grown and developed into bitter torture, had not the thought floated to me on the waves that I, too, would soon ebb and vanish in this fashion" (V, 214f.).

When Friedrich Schiller said, in his "Der Jüngling am Bache," "And thus my days, like the spring, flee without a pause," he, too, connected flowing water with the fugacity of man's life. Yet his use of the image is altogether different from Lenau's. Schiller's brook is a simple, one-plane equivalent, a poetic conceit, whereas Lenau's river is an image in depth. In his poem the rhetorical association of life and river—an end in itself in Schiller's poem—is but the starting point for Lenau's probe of the psyche. As the poem progresses, the connection between water and soul establishes itself more profoundly, and finally the poet's grief and the river become one symbolic unity. In the first stanza, man is still removed from the water and sees it is an outsider. It is a poetic version of the first sentence from the quoted letter to Sophie. In the second stanza, through the effective repetition of "hinein" (meaning "into it"), the connection is strengthened. The poet appears to project his individuality into the passing water: "O! starre nur hinein, hinein" ("Oh, go on staring into it"). In the next stanza, staring into the flowing river causes his eyes to weep. This is both a valid physiological observation and a significant symbolic development. The flowing tears and the flowing water, eventually merging, turn the motion into a symbol that acquires autonomy. In the last stanza, the motion takes on a consoling quality. Passing away is depicted as a healing of the heart's wounds:

Hinträumend wird Vergessenheit
Des Herzens Wunde schließen;
Die Seele sieht mit ihrem Leid
Sich selbst vorüberfließen.
(I, 537)

("Lost in dreaming, oblivion will close the heart's wound. The soul will see itself flow past, along with its sorrows.")

Early in his career, transiency had meant to Lenau a mere concept, and he expressed it in his first poems in the rhetorical idiom he had acquired from his models. Gradually the concept grew into an experience, and along with it the poet's verbal incisiveness became more acute. His imagination developed, and the area of his characteristic imagery defined itself. The motif of transiency grew with him. He applied it in never-ending variations and used it to create poetic symbols that far transcend the realm of the conceptual.

II *Turning Within*

Lenau cannot be called a universal poet. There are many areas of human experience he did not enter as a poet. His genius developed along one avenue only: the representation of the pensive, the mournful and, often, the oppressive. His phantasy embraced these aspects of life and established them as the substratum for his art.

In a letter to Karl Meyer, Lenau recalls a poem by Adelbert von Chamisso about a painter who nails a youth to the cross in order to see an authentic expression of the agony of death.[3] Lenau added that he would nail himself to the cross if this act would bring forth a good poem. Lenau was wont to disclaim his own existence in the service of art. He identified himself completely with his poems in the much-quoted statement: "I cannot call poetry a friend close to my heart; I think that I myself am poetry. Poetry is my selfest self" (III, 85).

By completely identifying himself with his works, Lenau had chosen to relinquish the objectivity and autonomy that most earlier poets had felt toward their work. Lenau maintained that his poems were direct emanations of his soul and he considered emotion and art identical. These are overstatements, to be sure, for no artist can create anything without being much aware of the formal, external aspects of his work, even though the creative impulse may at times result in a finished product without an apparent effort or even without an awareness on the part of the creator. In such a case, the perfection of the form was part of the "autonomous complex," in Jung's words, that matured within the artist and suddenly came to light, finished and complete. Whether or not Lenau labored at length over a given poem is really unimportant, notwithstanding the fact that some of his poems show definite traces of haste. What matters is that the only source on which Lenau drew for his poetic inspirations was his torn psyche and, at times, even its momentary mood. Many of his contemporaries, and even more so the poets of the Romantic age, created their works within a generally accepted frame of reference of spiritual and intellectual tenets. One critic, contrasting Lenau's imagery with that of Eichendorff, pointed out that Eichendorff's imagery relied on the secure grounds of his sincere religiosity, while Lenau's was conditioned by his tortured soul alone.[4] Eichendorff's poems express a religious transcendency which no longer meant anything to Lenau.

Lenau's receptive sensitivity toward subtle shades of his own emotions was both a blessing and a curse to him as a poet. On the one hand, the intensity of his mental tribulations made him search for and discover a realm of images and symbols conveying these tribulations that had not been tapped by any other poet. Expressing the confined area of his inner life, he created verbal equivalents that, in their haunting and, at times, surrealistic quality, point far into the future. He pushed his imagination along one avenue and drove himself far ahead of his time. On the other hand, he was prone to consider a rhymed record of his personal sufferings a form of literary art, mistaking his private self for the poetic self.

Searching for verbal equivalents of his innermost experiences which are, by their very nature, on a pre-verbal level, Lenau chose, at times, to portray landscapes and scenes that were not reflections of an outer reality but came form deep within him. They were inner landscapes, or landscapes of the soul, although they show some characteristics of outer reality. In his portrayal of inner landscapes, Lenau antedated Rilke. Landscapes of the soul are frequently encountered in Rilke's poems. His "Orpheus. Eurydike. Hermes" depicts the classical underworld in images that also pertain to the soul of the individual: "This is the wondrous mine of the souls. . . ." And, in a late fragmentary poem, he spoke of "the mountains of the heart" on which man is exposed.[5] The higher the region, the more impossible it becomes to establish a relationship with one's own existence. Not until sixty years after Lenau's death did a visible image of an inner self as a principle of artistic creation become a device generally accepted by the Expressionist painters.

Landscapes of the soul need not be surrealistic. The concepts of the real and unreal and their dim dividing line do not apply here. In "Ohne Wunsch" (I, 327) the poet tells his sweetheart that their love is doomed because all joys in his heart have died. Thus far, the poem contains nothing beyond a conventional metaphor of little interest. But Lenau extended the metaphor in the next two lines in such a way that it results in an autonomous image:

An den Bahren könnten wir
Nur mit Grauen Hochzeit halten.

("Our wedding feast, celebrated at the biers [of the dead joys] would be a dreadful one.")

In the last stanza, Lenau pictures one of his favorite inner scenes:

Ein zu trüber Lebensgang
Führte mich an steile Ränder,
Kind, mir würde um dich bang,
Flieh, es krachen die Geländer!
(I, 327)

("A too desolate course of life has led me to deep abysses. Child, I would fear for you. Flee, the railing is splintering!")

Existence at the brink of an abyss is an image that Lenau evoked again and again to convey his inner situation.[6] It does not signify a violent end, for there is no reference to a fall into the chasm. Man is in a precarious situation, unable to leave or even move. He is at the edge of his existence, afraid and desperate. Paradoxically, there is a frightful sense of permanence in this threatened existence. The image of man at the abyss has been shown to be an illustration not only of Lenau's inner situation, but also of the beliefs of Existentialism. Many parallels have been drawn between Lenau's poetry and the writings of Sören Kierkegaard.[7]

The poem, "Der trübe Wandrer" (I, 25), illustrates well how Lenau, starting out with an almost conventional metaphor and extending it, arrives at an image of an inner landscape. The initial metaphor is "the shores of life":

> Am Strand des Lebens irr ich, starre düster
> Ins Todesmeer, umhüllt von Nebelflor;

("I wander lost along the shores of life and stare gloomily into the sea of death which is shrouded in mist.")

The situation is related to the abyss image. In the remaining lines, the rhetorical concepts "shores of life" and "sea of death" are expanded into an imaginary scene. As the poet walks along the shore, he encounters various phantoms from his life. Teasing shadows of past hours of love flutter by, and funeral wreaths of the beloved dead are carried past him in the storm. A crucifix, in front of which he used to pray when a child, lies broken on the shore, washed over by the waves of death. He believes that he hears voices, from time to time, but they give way to silence, and again only the waves can be heard. The poet is accompanied by a "solemn friend" who points down at the dark waters and draws ever closer to him. The last line is an appeal to this friend: "Umarme mich, du stiller Todesmut!" ("Embrace me, thou quiet death urge!")

In the double sonnet "Einsamkeit" Lenau sees himself on a heath, alone and forsaken. In his despair, he tries to establish contact with inanimate objects:

> Warst du auf einer Heide so allein,
> So weißt du auch, wies einen dann bezwingt,
> Daß er umarmend stürzt an einen Stein;
>
> Daß er, von seiner Einsamkeit erschreckt,
> Entsetzt empor vom starren Felsen springt
> Und bang dem Winde nach die Arme streckt.
> (I, 304)

("If you ever were thus alone on a heath, you know how something forces you to throw yourself against a stone, embracing it; and, frightened by your solitude, to jump up from the barren rock in horror and stretch your arms out to the winds.")

So far, the lines convey a true or imagined gesture of tortuous solitude. In the second sonnet, however, the image of the heath loses its connotations of reality. It becomes apparent that the heath is not a factual location serving as a background to the poet's emotions. The heath is within the poet; it is the image of an inner reality. Wind and stone reject the wanderer, and so do roses, preoccupied with their own dying:

> Geh weiter: überall grüßt dich Verderben
> In der Geschöpfe langen dunklen Gassen;

("Go on your way. Destruction will greet you everywhere in the long dark alleys of all creatures".)

These alleys, not mentioned before, may be near the heath or part of it; or the poet's imagination may have focused on a different location altogether. The next three lines introduce an apocalyptic image:

> Siehst hier und dort sie aus den Hütten schauen,
> Dann schlagen sie vor dir die Fenster zu,
> Die Hütten stürzen, und du fühlst ein Grauen.
> (I, 305)

("Here and there you can see them, looking out from their huts. Then they bang the windows shut before you. The huts collapse, and you feel horror.")

What alleys are these? Who are the people in the huts, throwing their windows shut? Why do the huts collapse? They are not, and cannot be, real. They exist in the poet's imagination only. At this point, where the surrealistic elements become preponderant, one realizes that the heath, the rock, the wind and the roses were not part of a straight-forward, realistic setting either. They were aspects of the poet's inner landscape. The throwing shut of windows is an image of rejection, more drastic than the repulsion experienced from the rock and the wind, but not principally different. A new dimension is introduced into the poem with the image of the collapsing huts. Those who have rejected are now being destroyed, by a force that is unknown and irrational. The horror man experiences is no longer a simple consequence of his solitude, but it is also brought on by his inability to comprehend himself and the world around him. The experience of exclusion has reached its ultimate stage. The last three lines of the poem pose a question:

> Lieblos und ohne Gott! der Weg ist schaurig,
> Der Zugwind in den Gassen kalt; und du? –

Die ganze Welt ist zum Verzweifeln traurig.
(I, 305)

("Without love, and without a God; The path is dreadful, the drafty winds in the alleys blow cold; and what of you? Sadness and despair pervade the world.")

"Without love and without a God." This is the specific solitude the poet tried to capture in words and images. The question "And you?" is not answered. Man remains in a limbo, be it that he is eternally perched at the edge of a precipice or that he has no answer to a question touching upon the meaning of his existence. This is man's situation, as Lenau experienced it. The formulation that he gave to the experience of solitude explores the very core of this sensation. It is important that Lenau used strikingly modern images, not Romantic ones, in this instance. The phantastic, nightmarish character of the first tercet is most unusual for the literature of Lenau's time. The emotion underlying the poem must have been so genuine and intense that it made Lenau seek out new stylistic devices and new images. In grasping the essence of solitude as a violent, though unreal and traumatic experience, Lenau was far ahead of his time. In effect, the poem is a sharp renunciation of the motif of solitude as seen by Eichendorff and other Romantic poets—an act of introspection that leads to the prospect of ultimate values, and furthers artistic creation.

The span of Lenau's artistic performance is great. From the imitative images, derived from the works of outdated models, it stretches to the symbolic expression of the most urgent, profound, and timeless questions in man's existence.

CHAPTER 3

Approaches to Nature: The Perfection of the Poetic Symbol

I *The Symbolic View of Nature*

IF one were to search for motifs that persist in Lenau's works, nature would emerge as the most predominant one. It would, in fact, be difficult to find more than a dozen poems in which nature plays no part. In November, 1831, after having set out on his trip to Germany, Lenau wrote to Schurz:

> The contemplation of human life in its many aspects is to me the most fascinating thing, after the fascination that nature holds for me. Nature will always be my dearest friend, and human life is nothing but the image of nature as it is reflected on the agitated waves of our instincts. (III, 85)

To a large extent, this viewpoint is shared by many Romantic poets. Lenau had fully subscribed to the Romantic theory of poetry and even gone beyond it. When he saw nature as it appears on the agitated waves of our instincts, he reflected an attitude that had prevailed in Romanticism from its very beginning. It is often referred to as "Naturgefühl," a feeling for or in nature, and can be defined as a projection of human emotions into the realm of nature.

Lenau's views were strongly influenced by the philosopher Schelling, whose works he had studied. In his *Philosophy of Nature,* Schelling refers to nature as an undeveloped, unconscious intelligence, an embryo of the mind (*Geist*). Nature comprises a series of intellectual levels, which ultimately reach the realm of the "Geist." Later on, especially in his *Philosophy of Identity,* Schelling was not far from Goethe's classical view when he maintained that nature and *Geist* are essentially the same. Since nature possesses the same creativity that is characteristic of the "Geist," there can be no difference between that which is inside and that which is outside of human consciousness. This viewpoint was subscribed to by Hegel as well,[1] and Lenau expressed similar ideas when he wrote to Emilie Reinbeck in 1833 that "the formative power of artistic phantasy and the formative power of nature are one and the same, and the creative artist, so to speak, carries within his soul the spiritual complement of visible creations" (III, 234).

To some extent, Lenau's views represent typically the Romanticists' attitude toward nature. Like all Romanticists, he cared little for detailed observation of the external world. His main object was the creation of an atmosphere, and he considered nature a receptacle for his own emotions rather than an object of study.[2] Within this general attitude, Lenau ventured on new paths of nature poetry. He was fully aware of being an innovator in the use of nature symbolism. In 1839, in a conversation with Max Löwenthal, he said:

> The area in which I have achieved something new in German literature and in which no one matches me, no matter how many imitators have appeared, is my nature poetry, my poetic penetration and reflection of nature, of its relationship to man, and of its struggle toward the "Geist."[3]

Lenau held certain views on the function of nature in poetry that go beyond the adoption of the principle of ascribing human feelings to inanimate nature, or the "pathetic fallacy," as John Ruskin called it. There are two critical statements by Lenau: one in a review of a volume of poetry by one Georg Keil; the other in a letter to Schurz. Both illuminate Lenau's poetic intention. In the review, written in 1834, Lenau expressed his dissatisfaction with the nature poems by Keil (who has long since been forgotten). He maintained that Keil lacked all the characteristics of the modern age and seemed to belong to an older era of German literature, since his poetry either enumerated disconnected natural phenomena or drew parallels between an aspect of human life and a corresponding event in nature. Lenau continued:

> But neither a sterile enumeration nor a merely rational parallelism should, strictly speaking, be called an "artistic presentation." True nature poetry, it seems to me, must bring nature and human life into close conflict. From this conflict a third, organic element must spring, which should be a symbol of a higher spiritual unity that includes both nature and human life. (VI, 33)

It is obvious that Lenau had in mind a truly symbolic view of man and nature, and the presentation of an element that underlies the phenomena of both man and nature. Many, although not most of Lenau's own nature poems fulfill this requirement. It can be said that he never indulged in a "sterile enumeration" of natural phenomena. But often he drew parallels between nature and man, a technique cultivated by the Swabian Poets. They exerted a strong influence on Lenau in this respect. In the quoted review, Lenau paraphrased a poem by Keil, "Die Tränen," and rejected it as a series of reasoned parallels: The glowing summer earth finds refreshment in rain; the human heart, burning with pain, is comforted by tears. Yet many of Lenau's own poems, although they are emotionally determined, proceed in similar allegorical parallels.

In the letter to Schurz, written shortly after the review, Lenau criticized the imagery of the Swabian Poet Karl Mayer. He took Mayer to task for roaming through the forest with the intent of finding a possible approach to nature, for a "weak spot" where he could "get at her." In this manner, Lenau continued, the poet confines himself too much to the outer material world. He lies in wait for natural phenomena, which he then puts to work in a poem in a superficial way.

> A poet should create within himself and from within himself. External nature which should supply him with certain media, must function only in his recollection, although the recollection has to become a productive image in the moment of the poet's creative activity. In short, the visually perceived natural phenomenon, having become a symbol, should never be the end in itself, but merely a means toward the presentation of a poetic idea. (III, 270)

By "poetic idea," Lenau obviously did not mean an abstract, rational concept that should be illustrated and exemplified through a poetic image. Such a procedure would be purely allegorical. He thought of a spiritual matter that is not rationally and conceptually conveyable. He called it a "poetic" idea because it does not exist before it is given expression through a poetic device and cannot be expressed in any other fashion. A simple, non-poetic idea would be the equality of all men, for example. But the oppressive atmosphere that is conveyed, for example, in Goethe's poem "Meeresstille" is a poetic idea. It would be difficult or impossible to describe it in any other fashion, to abstract and categorize it. The verbal structure which transmits a poetic idea is a symbol. The term "symbol" will not be used here in the sense of an extended metaphor.

It is not an expression that refers to something else and receives meaning only when its reference is correctly understood. A literary symbol does not point to anything other than itself. It does not refer; it exists. As in Goethe's poem, it immediately establishes itself as the universal form of what it expresses, as an archetype.

Following his own theoretical insight into the nature of nature symbolism, Lenau wrote a number of truly symbolic poems that convey a "poetic idea," but he also did exactly what he criticized in Mayer's work: He went to "spy" on nature and sought out phenomena to be used for parallels between nature and man. An all-important aspect of Lenau's nature poetry is his emotional attitude toward nature. Unlike many other Romantic poets, he did not look upon nature as an invariable source of comfort. In his hypersensitivity, he was troubled by nature's fickleness and sovereign neglect of the individual.[4] Although he professed to see in nature a manifestation of metaphysical knowledge and eternal truth, the subjectivity of his outlook made the outer realm a potential projection of his inner self, and he found his own emotions reflected in all phenomena of the physical world. Communing with nature meant, to most Romantic poets, an attempt to lose their selves in it, to become part of a greater entity, and to catch a glimpse of the transcendental realms that they considered part of nature. Not so Lenau. He saw in nature mostly a visible extension of his self. In his eyes, it harbored a wide range of emotional attitudes, from unbound gaiety to abysmal torture, with a strong emphasis on the gloomier aspects. In its relationship to man, nature was, to Lenau, everything from a sympathetic refuge for the individual's sorrows to a force so blind, brutal, and devastating that man could never make peace with it. His blithe scenes of nature usually lack depth and have the ring of artificiality. His threatening and melancholy images of nature are more genuine. More and more, nature became to Lenau an expression of his own propensity toward themes of death and transiency. He wrote to Sophie Schwab that his poetry was bound to sound "monotonous" (an accusation levelled by Gustav Schwab) because of his submission to nature, which, in turn, conveyed to him an "attitude of melancholy expiration" (III, 134).

II *The Human Element in Nature*

In examining the stylistic function which nature actually exercises in Lenau's poems, three levels of increasing subtlety will be discerned. On the first level, nature serves as a background, a device to set a scene and create an atmosphere. This category is significant in an investigation of Lenau's motifs, for it shows what elements of nature attracted him most. On the second level, man and nature are brought together more closely. Nature serves as a conveyer of human feelings, and human traits and feelings are ascribed to it. On the third level, symbols are encountered. No longer are there any parallels drawn between the spheres of man and nature, but both are fused into one. In these poems, "poetic ideas" which have to do with a subtle blending of the inner and the outer world are expressed in symbols.

Quantitatively, it would be difficult to do justice to the first category. Almost all of Lenau's epic poems and ballads are set against a background of somber or terrifying landscapes. The association of this background with the action depicted has a catalytic effect. It is usually the stormy night that embodies the elements of horror, destruction, and death.

The lack of colors in Lenau's poems is conspicuous. Faust, a genuinely Lenauesque character, denounces colorful nature. The "green rubbish" causes his heart to ache (II, 80). Lenau's autumn poems are kept in a dark grey or black, or they appear without color altogether. Night scenes abound. To Emilie Reinbeck, Lenau described his condition as "amphimelas," black all around (V, 150). In "Bitte" (I, 15), the solace of night and its magical dark brings death or at least mental extinction. It is a symbol of relief from the woes of this earth. These and many other examples show that Lenau's enthusiasm for the night—a prevalent Romantic attitude—was more like that of Nietzsche than of Novalis to whom night was the entrance to the secrets of the universe.

The second category, images of personified nature, covers an area as broad as the first. It begins with unsubtle instances of "pathetic fallacy," such as moaning forests and crying brooks, and ends short of attaining true symbols. Lenau vivified small details in nature, but there are also large-scale images, such as a vaguely anthropomorphous "Mother Nature."

Images of water animation are especially interesting since they show most clearly Lenau's intention to create new myths, an ambition common to most Romantic poets. According to a report by a friend of Lenau, he considered it one of the poet's functions to invent myths and legends that are as profound, naïve, and powerful as if the "Volk," the collective unconscious of a people, had invented them.[5] Lenau maintained that he seriously believed in mermaids (III, 194), as did the nature philosopher Gotthilf Heinrich Schubert. In "Die Seejungfrauen" (I, 145), which is reminiscent of Heine's "Seegespenst," the poet feels the urge to plunge to the bottom of the sea. However, while Heine is attracted by one particular maiden in the sunken city down below, Lenau wants to watch the mermaids dance in the twilight of the sea. Heine's "death wish" is, in fact, a yearning for life at the side of his lost beloved. His sunken city appears bathed in sunlight. Lenau's urge to plunge into the sea is a genuine death wish. The mermaids remain distant and impersonal, and the poet would cower silently and undetected in the eternally misty twilight of the deep.

Water conveys a rich gamut of dolor and despair in Lenau's poems. It can express a yearning for self-destruction ("The rapids rush toward the great fall, as if torn along by yearning for annihilation," in "Niagara" [I, 272]); it may suggest fear ("With a frightened cry, the spring gushes from a dark gate in the rock," in "Einsamkeit" [I, 95]); and it may express various kinds of sorrow: A brook passes by, weeping ("Die Werbung" [I, 157]), wails in loneliness ("Täuschung" [I, 316]), flows past lamenting ("Die Waldkapelle" [I, 166]), or surges by, wild and embittered (*Savonarola,* II, 192). It may convey reproach ("An mein Vaterland" [I, 150]) and disgust ("Ahasver, der ewige Jude" [I, 77]).

Humanized nature images are usually extended metaphors or allegories. They have sprung from a particular way of conceptual thinking rather than from a strong poetic imagination. However, there are many instances where Lenau ascribed characteristics from the human realm to nature. In "Ein Herbstabend" he described the flight of wild geese to the South, predicting that the South would not be a safe abode for them. Death has spread its nets there, too. Then he connects the geese's cries with nature's attempts to escape pervading death:

Natur das Ewge schaut in unruhvollen Träumen,
Fährt auf und will entfliehn den todverfallnen Räumen.

Der abgerißne Ruf, womit Zugvögel schweben,
Ist Aufschrei wirren Traums von einem ewgen Leben.
(I, 282)

("Nature, in restless dreams, envisions the eternal, starts up and wishes to escape from the doomed realm. The broken call which migratory birds emit is a cry out of a confused dream of eternal life.")

The image of nature, dreaming uneasily, carries vaguely anthropomorphous connotations, without being allegorical. But the foremost impression the poem conveys is one of great expanse. The image of a restless, tossing sleeper—there is a definite pathological undertone—is enlarged and projected into a vast realm. The whole universe becomes identified with the restless sleeper.

Lenau was fond of using such expansive and, at times, surrealistic images. The prime example is the "Sturmesmythe." The poem goes back, supposedly, to an actual observation Lenau made on Long Island Sound.[6] Sea and clouds are personified. At first, the sea appears silent and motionless, as if dead, its "wavepulse" barely perceptible. Then dark clouds, daughters of the ocean, hurriedly draw near in "stormy oppressedness" and gather anxiously around the silent sleeper's couch, speaking in thunders, flashing their lightning glances, raining down their grief, and wondering if their aged mother, the sea, is dead. But the daughters' concern wakes the sea, and she rises up:

Mutter – Kinder – brausend sich umschlingen,
Und sie tanzen freudenwild und singen
Ihrer Lieb ein Lied im Sturmeschor.
(I, 277)

("Mother, children, embrace each other in a roar, and they dance wild with joy, and they sing together a stormy chorus to their love.")

The poem presents a mythological picture of a storm gathering and breaking and, at the same time, retains a framework of true observation and meteorological fact. There is a remarkable crescendo in the poem, an almost musical movement from the quiet opening with sunset, calm water, and approaching night (not without an ominous undertone) to the suddenly unleashed fury of rising wind and waves. One could imagine a painting of the scene by Blake or a Surrealist.

Lenau's predilection for expansive images, such as nature itself or the ocean and clouds, for the portrayal of emotions forms a special category of celestial or cosmic images. One would try in vain to find definite ideas or functions in any of them—clouds, thunder, lightning, the sky, the sun, stars, and the moon. They are associated with joy, pleasure, sorrow, despair and all the other states of mind that are transmitted by small-scale terrestrial nature images. Their manifestation in such immense forms as celestial objects lends to this group of nature poems the force of mythical actions and passions.

In some instances, celestial images are used to intensify human emotions. For example, in "Gewitter" (I, 533) man's tribulations are clothed in metaphors of celestial phenomena. The clear sky of the soul is heavy with angry thoughts; the star of the eye flashes ominously; evening glow radiates in the eye, and the clouds have dissolved. Although such metaphors are not free of a certain contrived quality, the poem makes a strong impact because of the superhuman qualities given to the emotions. In other instances, celestial bodies are ascribed human attributes: Thunder grumbles from the depth of the sky's breast ("Ziska" [I, 432]); heaven's sinister, silent countenance awaits a storm ("Zwei Polen" [I, 247]); the sky seems to mourn (*Die Albigenser* [II, 382]; and weep upon a grave ("An einem Grabe" [I, 405]).

The most prominent example of cosmic imagery in Lenau's works is the poem "Himmelstrauer." As so often, Lenau used characteristics from the human realm to describe tellurian phenomena, but the two elements are blended so successfully that the final effect goes beyond a mere intensification of a cosmic picture through human attributes. There is the indication that a third entity, or, in Lenau's own words, "a symbol of that higher spiritual unity that includes both nature and human life" (VI, 33) could arise from a perfect balance of human and natural phenomena that was nearly achieved in this poem:

Am Himmelsantlitz wandelt ein Gedanke,
Die düstre Wolke dort, so bang, so schwer;
Wie auf dem Lager sich der Seelenkranke,
Wirft sich der Strauch im Winde hin und her.

Vom Himmel tönt ein schwermutmattes Grollen,
Die dunkle Wimper blinzet manches Mal,
— So blinzen Augen, wenn sie weinen wollen, —
Und aus der Wimper zuckt ein schwacher Strahl. —

Nun schleichen aus dem Moore kühle Schauer
Und leise Nebel übers Heideland;

> Der Himmel ließ, nachsinnend seiner Trauer,
> Die Sonne lässig fallen aus der Hand.
>
> (I, 64)

("A thought is crossing the countenance of heaven, the somber cloud, there, so woeful and heavy; like a person sick at heart [lit.: a psychopath] tossing on his bed, the bush tosses to and fro in the wind. A melancholy and tired muttering sounds the sky. The dark eyelash blinks a few times like eyes on the verge of tears, and a pale ray flickers from the eyelash. Chills and slow mists move stealthily from the moors across the health; heaven, pondering its own sorrow, heedlessly lets the sun drop out of its hand.")

The fine blending is achieved partly through the choice of words. "Wandelt" in the first and "schleichen" in the ninth line usually pertain to the realm of man, but their transferral to nature is less conspicuous than in a metaphor such as "the weeping forest" which Lenau was fond of using. The picture of the sleepless psychopath tossing on his bed, the despair and chill that are creeping up in the moment of final indifference—all unmistakably Lenauesque ideas and sentiments—make for a definite impression that pertains to the human sphere. The reader tends to forget that Lenau was actually writing about nature. The idea of a higher unity of man and nature comes across clearly in this poem. It is a true "poetic idea" Lenau is dealing with, and the finished poem is marred only slightly by the unfortunate choice of certain words, such as "blinzen" and "lässig," which detract from the cosmic atmosphere of the poem. It is striking that the sun is given no individual value at all and is casually dropped by the sky (or heaven). The image of the center and life of the galaxy being dropped by a sky which reflects upon its sorrows represents what one could call an apocalyptic view of melancholy.

Among all celestial bodies, the moon is dearest to Lenau. Aside from many instances where it is used in the traditional Romantic setting of the night, it may also suggest death and transiency. It is an evil and insidious thing in "Robert und der Invalide" (I, 65), where it steals away sleep with its silvery fingers. Lenau used one moon image repeatedly and with symbolic significance, that of moonlight reflected on water. To him, moonlight and water were in secret communication ("Die Seejungfrauen" [I, 145]). Moonlight may tremble, rest, or play on water, as for example in *Faust*:

Hell scheint der Mond, es spielen, leisen Bebens,
Die Strahlen lieblich auf dem tiefen See,
Wie über den Geheimnissen des Lebens
Und seiner Tiefe ungeahntem Weh
Die Kinderseelen lieblich zitternd spielen,
Die rein und klar vom Himmel niederfielen.
(II, 61)

("The moon is bright; its beams, trembling gently, play upon the deep lake as the souls of children, descended from heaven purely and radiantly, hover above the secrets of life and the unimagined woes of its depths.")

The comparison is subtle and adds significance to both the nature scene and the thought of the children's souls.

III *Reaching for the Balance*

The third category of Lenau's nature images comprises symbols, archetypes, or primordial images. They are not part of metaphors, similes, or comparisons and do not rationally convey an analogous object or event. Primordial images transmit an inimitable, irrational impact that is the very essence of poetry. In his poems renouncing love, Lenau came closest to, or actually succeeded in, creating true nature symbols. In "Traurige Wege," a Sophie poem, a definitely symbolic atmosphere can be observed. The subject matter is simple. The poet and his beloved are seen in three settings. They go through a lovely green forest, float in a boat down a river by moonlight, and walk through a churchyard on a windy dismal day. Their love finds security (*Halt*) in none of the three, not even in the churchyard:

An den Kreuzen, an den Steinen
Fand die Liebe keinen Halt;
Sahen uns die Toten weinen,
Als wir dort vorbeigewallt?
(I, 287)

("Our love found no abode by the crosses and tombstones; did the dead see us weep, as we passed by?")

The poem contains images of transciency, of time and happiness passing. It primarily transmits movement. "Wege" is in the title. The atmosphere of the poem is determined by the verbal expressions *gehen* (go), *entfliehen* (flee), *fahren* (move), *vorüberrinnen* (drift past), *keinen Halt finden* (find no place to stay), and *vorbeiwallen* (pass). In this poem, Lenau gave to his love such dimensions as exceed verbal classification. The image of love passing through the various scenes gives it a quality of dejection and yet a serene, detached beauty that would be difficult to express in rational terms.

Two short poems will further illustrate the distinction between symbolic and non-symbolic poetry. In "Bitte," reminiscent of Goethe's "Über allen Gipfeln," Lenau beseeches the night to cast its spell on him forever:

Weil auf mir, du dunkles Auge,
Übe deine ganze Macht,
Ernste, milde, träumerische,
Unergründlich süße Nacht!

Nimm mit deinem Zauberdunkel
Diese Welt von hinnen mir,
Daß du über meinem Leben
Einsam schwebest für und für.
(I, 15)

("Rest upon me, you dark eye, exercise your whole power, earnest, mild, dreamy, ineffably sweet night! Take from me, with your magic darkness, this world, so that you may hover above my life, forever and ever.")

The poem is purged of anything accidental pertaining to a definite situation. The poet has ceased to be the mouthpiece of a momentary mood that he feels urged to communicate to the reader. His own person stands invisibly in the background, has dropped all temporal impulses, and seems to be the mere instrument of a voice coming from the depths that only poets can sound. There is only one metaphor: The night is called "dark eye." This image is not a simple pathetic fallacy, an ascribing of human traits to inanimate nature; it is more subtle. Lenau crystallized the physical, realistic experience of the night's darkness into a haunting image of magical, hypnotic power. By virtue of speaking of one eye only, he gave the image a surrealistic quality. Technically, it belongs to the category of Lenau's expansive, celestial images, but its potency is unique. The eye image holds something fearsome, enchanting, and enslaving that transcends the benevolent night-mother image used by Novalis. And yet Lenau called it "mild" and "sweet." It is sweet to him in the desired effect of freeing him from the world. A similar, though less profound motif was encountered in "Himmelstrauer," where an imaginary eye hides behind the dark eyelashes of the clouds.

In "Nebel," Lenau pursued an aim similar to that in "Bitte":

Du, trüber Nebel, hüllest mir
Das Tal mit seinem Fluß,
Den Berg mit seinem Waldrevier
Und jeden Sonnengruß.

Nimm fort in deine graue Nacht
Die Erde weit und breit!
Nimm fort, was mich so traurig macht,
Auch die Vergangenheit!

(I, 33)

("Dismal mist, you have veiled the valley and its river, the mountain with its woods, and every greeting of the sun. Take away into your gray night all of the earth! Take what makes me so sad; take also the past!")

The shroud of fog in this poem takes the place of the night in "Bitte." But the poet's words do not come from similar depths. The range is shorter, and the poet himself is considerably more in the foreground. The diction does not transmit an air of mythical perpetuity and completeness. Compounds like "Waldrevier" and "Sonnengruss" are clichés traceable to Hölty. "Bitte" has great tonal beauty and is a fervent prayer of beautifully sustained quality. "Nebel" remains earthbound and is almost an utterance of annoyance. If the mist blots out things I like, why can it not hide what pains me—the world and the past? In the last two lines especially, the poet refers to his own sorrows and to his own life, thus expecting the reader to focus his attention on Lenau rather than the poem.

Nature symbols clearly do not come about merely because a poet has established an external connection between nature and man. If the two are drawn together solely by a series of comparisons, the result may be a set of unusual images and metaphors, without necessarily conveying a poetic effect. As Lenau himself had realized, a more profound element underlying both man and nature is needed to make a poetic idea come to life. He devised a verbal image for what he considered the essence in nature, that which synthesizes and gives meaning to all its manifestations: the "nature spirits" (*Naturgeister*). He regarded them as the epitome of the secret behind all external phenomena and considered them creatures of a realm germane to symbols and primordial images. They have human characteristics. Attempting, in the poem "Beethovens Büste" (I, 413), to describe Beethoven's music through visual images, Lenau characterized it as "songs the nature spirit whispers into the first dreams of a beautiful child." Disregarding the fact that he was speaking about music, Lenau, it is noteworthy, connected the utterances of the nature spirit with dreams of a child. Both dreams and children are traditionally associated with things primordial, and modern psychology tends to support this viewpoint.

Nature spirits sing in the poem "Am Grabe eines Schwermütigen, der sich selbst den Tod gegeben" (I, 416).[7] The eulogized dead has heard the most dismal of the spirits' songs and has tried to sing it again. Now "this heart," as Lenau calls the dead poet in a characteristic synecdoche, has perfected the song and burst at the same time. The poet's ability to hear the spirits' song has destroyed him. It is implied that only very few "hearts" can hear the song, as there are very few poets who can perceive the archetypal or universal in nature. Lenau believed that those who are able will perish through the experience. They crucify themselves for the sake of art.

IV *"Schilflieder"*

The "Schilflieder" are, without a doubt, Lenau's supreme achievements in the creation of nature symbols. They are products of a relatively early period (1832), of a time still unburdened by his love for Sophie Löwenthal. It would be difficult to say what the five poems in this cycle "are about." About nature? Or a girl? Both subjects are in the poems, but they appear as one. Lenau achieved a perfect balance between the realms of man and nature. The beloved is distant; the landscape is of a stylized paleness. It is characterized by willows, a pond, by turns calm and agitated, sunset, weeping willows, rushes, clouds, rain, lightning, stars, the moon, a forest path, stags. The auditory images include the voice of the beloved, the wind, and waterfowl.

These images are not unique in Lenau's poems; they are, on the whole, among the poet's most common. He almost seems to have made an effort to bring together his favorite sense impressions. A good number of the motifs and images occur in poems written shortly before the "Schilflieder." In "Reiseempfindung" (I, 5), the moonlight seems to be clinging to birch trees; and in the fifth "Schilflied" the rushes are intertwined with the light of the moon. In "Das Mondlicht" (I, 11) a link is established between a girl and the light reflected in the water. In the first "Schilflied" the thought of the distant beloved is compared to the reflected image of the evening star. The motif recurs in the fourth "Schilflied": Lightning is mirrored in the pond, and the image of the beloved appears to the poet. As in the "Schilflieder," the poet feels the presence of the beloved during a stormy night, near a body of water, in "Nächtliche Wanderung" (I, 12). The change of scenery from the gold of the evening sun to a stormy night, with the beloved occupying the poet's thoughts, occurs in "Meine Braut" (I, 16) and, shortly thereafter, in the present cycle. The image of "pale roses" appears in the fifth "Schilflied" and in the earlier "Vergangenheit" (I, 27).

Although the cycle is not distinguished by novel images and motifs, it is incomparably superior to any of the poems mentioned. Lenau wrote the "Schilflieder" at a time of relative mental calm.[8] The intensity of these poems is not derived from a temporary emotion transformed into verse; it is an intensity that lies strictly within the realm of art.

The first poem begins with a nature description. The sun is setting, and the willows' branches droop into the deep, quiet pond. It contains the only direct comparison found between man and nature in the cycle:

In mein stilles, tiefes Leiden
Strahlst du, Ferne! hell und mild,
Wie durch Binsen hier und Weiden
Strahlt des Abendsternes Bild.
(I, 18)

("Into my quiet, deep sorrow you, my distant one, shine brightly and gently, as the image of the evening star shines through sedges and willows.")

The connection is a subtle one. It hinges on the word *strahlen* (radiate, shine), which is used metaphorically one time, and literally the other. The comparison between the thought of the beloved and the reflection of a star transcends the category of "pathetic fallacy" and material, physical properties; and the words "quiet, deep," here modifying the poet's sorrow, were used in the first stanza to describe the pond. The comparison had been carefully prepared.

The second poem portrays nature in a more agitated state. Clouds rush by, and rain falls. The lamenting winds no longer find the reflection of the star in the stormy lake. This observation is immediately followed by the lines "Deine Liebe lächelt nimmer / Nieder in mein tiefes Weh!" ("Your love no longer smiles down upon my deep woe.") No comparison is drawn, but the connection is understood without one. The reader still associates the thought of the beloved with the reflected evening star. Now both have become obscured. By not spinning out the comparison, a poetic element has been gained: a union, an almost complete identity, between the two ephemeral objects. The love of the distant woman now *is* the reflected starlight and can no longer avail the poet.

In the third poem, the atmosphere is calm again. The poet walks along the edge of the pond in the evening twilight and thinks of his beloved. As it grows darker, the sedges begin to rustle mysteriously. Their whispers bring the poet to the verge of tears. The sounds of the rushes are given significance in the last stanza:

Und ich mein, ich höre wehen
Leise deiner Stimme Klang
Und im Weiher untergehen
Deinen lieblichen Gesang.
(I, 19)

("And I think that I hear the soft sound of your voice waft by and your lovely singing die away in the pond.")

The poet did not expressly say that the sound of the rushes was the voice of the beloved. As in the preceding poem, the association is subtler than could be expressed in words, and Lenau intensified the interdependence of the two elements through his choice of verbs: The rushes, moved by the wind, "lament" and "whisper"—properties of the human sphere. And in the last stanza he hears the soft sound of the girl's voice *wehen* (literally, "blow, waft"), a verb usually ascribed to the motion and sound of the wind.

In terms of intensity and agitation, the fourth poem brings the cycle to a climax. The meter differs from that of the other four poems. It is a trochaic trimeter with catalectic endings, as compared with the tetrameter in the others. The first stanza is ominous, with latent intensity: The sun is down, a sultry wind blows, and black clouds are driven across the sky. The rest of the poem captures the unleashed fury of the forces of nature. Pale flashes of lightning chase across the sky and are reflected in the pond. The serenity of the first poem has given way to turbulence. The image of the beloved appears as in lightning flashes as part of the setting:

Wie gewitterklar
Mein ich dich zu sehn
Und dein langes Haar
Frei im Sturme wehn!
(I, 19)

("In what lightning brightness I seem to see you, with your long hair flying in the wind!")

The beloved, shown concretely through the image of her flying hair, is part of the agitated elements. Throughout the cycle, the reader is given only three details describing her: her smile, her voice, and her hair. All of these are parts of nature as well. This is especially true in the present instance. Her hair appears as something in common between her and nature. It flies in the storm and is part of nature as much as it is part of her. The vaguely surrealistic fashion in which the girl appears as part of the landscape throughout the first four poems is brought to a climax at this point.

The composition of the cycle follows along a line of *crescendi* and *decrescendi*. The first and third poems are calm; the second and, even more so, the fourth are agitated. In the last poem, one of the gems of German lyric poetry, absolute calm prevails:

Auf dem Teich, dem regungslosen,
Weilt des Mondes holder Glanz,
Flechtend seine bleichen Rosen
In des Schilfes grünen Kranz.

Hirsche wandeln dort am Hügel,
Blicken in die Nacht empor;
Manchmal regt sich das Geflügel
Träumerisch im tiefen Rohr.

Weinend muß mein Blick sich senken;
Durch die tiefste Seele geht
Mir ein süßes Deingedenken,
Wie ein stilles Nachtgebet!
(I, 20)

("On the motionless pond rests the moon's gentle sheen, interweaving its pale roses with the green wreath of the rushes. Deer stray on the hillside, looking up into the night; at times birds, dreaming, rustle in the tall reeds. I must lower my eyes, weeping; through the depth of my soul passes a tender thought of you like a quiet evening prayer.")

After the intense motion of the fourth poem, the cycle comes to a virtual standstill in the fifth. In the blending of the domains of man and nature, perfection is attained here. In the first four poems, an atmosphere was created by a nature image, and then the beloved, or the thought of her, appeared within this atmosphere. In the very first poem, the association was supported through a direct comparison, a device no longer needed in the second, third, and fourth poems. She and nature now form one unit and yield one uniform impression; but Lenau strengthens the unity, in the three middle poems, through technical devices other than comparisons. In the last poem, however, no detail of the diction points to the fact that landscape and girl are in any way related. It is not her image that enters the poem, as in the other poems, but merely a thought of her passes through the poet's soul. But the preceding poems have prepared the ground: The association is present here as much as before. For the third time in the cycle, Lenau uses the image of light reflected on the water. In his poetry, and especially in the "Schilflieder," this image is associated with the most tender emotions. In this instance, the reflected moonlight is referred to as "pale roses" that are interwoven with the green garland of the rushes. The domain of the imagery is feminine. The two verbs used in the first stanza, *weilen* and *flechten,* pertain vaguely to the human sphere, but their use in the present nature description is not startling. It merely opens vistas toward a more sublime poetic reality. The same applies to the adjective *bleich,* modifying "the roses."

The second stanza introduces animal life—deer and birds—as contrasted with the plant imagery of the first, and it is a further step in the direction toward the human realm. Goethe proceeded similarly in the imagery of his "Über allen Gipfeln" which takes us from mountain tops and tree tops to birds and man. Even without the four preceding poems, the fifth poem in itself aims toward the realm of man in the last stanza. In the end, when the poet's eyes overflow, it is not only because he is moved by the scenery, which was to him more than an invitation to commune with nature; it has evoked in him thoughts of his beloved. He appears entirely passive and receptive and does not consciously direct his thoughts toward her. All claim to her has been relinquished. The diction, at this point, is unusual. A very literal translation of the last two lines would be: "A sweet remembrance of you goes through my deepest soul." Thinking is normally a conscious act and requires an agent. Lenau turned it into a passive experience, a benediction received. He seems to be observing an autonomous act of thinking passing through him at the deepest level. The comparison with an evening prayer lends to the experience of love and yearning a religious connotation and also moves it into the realm of childhood and purity.

The cycle cannot be classified by such terms as "sorrowful" and "melancholy"; it is both, but it is also much more, for it carries a "poetic idea" that defies definition in conceptual terms and can be conveyed only in the form of the poems. The "Schilflieder" are about love, but not about a happy or an unhappy, a frustrated or a fulfilled love. They grasp the emotion itself at a level where such restrictive modifiers do not apply. The girl depicted in the poems attains an almost mythical stature. Her image, purged of all individual and specific attributes, has become the image of all women—a primordial image. A friend of Lenau's reports that the Stuttgart circle assumed that there was a definite reference in the "Schilflieder" to Lotte Gmelin—an unjustified, or at least irrelevant, thought—and thereafter called her "Schilflottchen."[9] There may be more significance to this nickname than Lenau's friends realized at the time. The term suggests a mythical figure and is reminiscent of sprites and water nymphs such as Fouqué's Undine. It pertains to a realm of archetypal images, a realm where symbols are born.

V *"Waldlieder"*

Lenau's second great cycle of nature poetry, the "Waldlieder," is a product of later years. Written in 1843 and early 1844, it forms the poet's last major lyric achievement before his breakdown. Like the "Schilflieder," the second cycle had been growing in his imagination for a long time before he actually wrote them. As early as 1837, Lenau mentioned the plan of a "Waldlied" to Sophie, telling her in a note that it was impossible for him to write it without her. "Dejected as I am, things present themselves to me fleeting and nebulous" (IV, 82). Then, and in the following years, Lenau could not find the mental and emotional peace needed for the project. He was preoccupied with theological and philosophical problems and, above all, with his love for Sophie. Even when he did find the desired peace and set out to compose the cycle, he could not keep it free from direct allusions to Sophie and references to Hegel's philosophy. As one critic has stated, Lenau freed himself in this cycle "of the numerous poetical errors of the past decade";[10] nevertheless, the intellectual matters he was concerned with were reflected directly in the cycle.

The cycle, consisting of nine poems, is more than five times the length of the "Schilflieder." Compared with the "Waldlieder," the "Schilflieder" are pure nature poetry. In the late cycle, Lenau found it necessary to redefine his attitude toward nature. In previous years, he had renounced nature as capricious, indifferent, and cruel. Now he turned back to her as his ultimate refuge. What had not been an issue at the time of the "Schilflieder"—the poet's own views on the relationship between man and nature—had, in the meantime, become problematical to Lenau. Love plays an altogether different part in the "Waldlieder" from what it did in the "Schilflieder." The experience of love had been wholly converted into poetry in the early cycle, whereas, in the later one, Lenau's passion for Sophie Löwenthal is evident in its external reality. The poet sent the entire cycle to her, but to Emilie Reinbeck he sent only poems one, two, four, six, and nine. He may have withheld from Emilie poems five and seven because of their relative difficulty, but poems three and eight were kept from her because they contain patent allusions to Sophie, which Emilie would have easily detected.

While, in the "Schilflieder," Lenau had achieved a synthesis of man and nature by implication and form, he resorted to the devices of analogy and direct comparison in the "Waldlieder." There are instances of plain pathetic fallacy, for example the description of a storm: The thunder is as great as if the sky were trying to smash itself against the rocks (I, 447). Such inadequacies make the "Waldlieder" a less closely knit and less homogeneous work of art than the "Schilflieder." The poet assumes a more central part and a more problematic, intellectual position than in the earlier cycle. In view of this fact, the question arises whether the "Waldlieder" have any poetic symbols to offer or are an example of Lenau's thought-ridden monologues in verse. The poet himself supplied the answer. He introduced into the cycle a figure, Merlin, that functions as a "nature spirit," a mediator between man and nature. Through him the poems reach a realm more significant than the conceptual problems in them would allow. The legendary figure of Merlin, the half-demented Welsh magician and prophet, was a favorite with many Romantic poets and had always been closely connected with the forces of nature.[11] There is a ballad by Ludwig Uhland, "Merlin der Wilde," which Lenau undoubtedly knew. In Uhland's poem, the nature prophet hears in the rustling of the forest at night the *Geist der Welt*, the spirit and essence of the world. To Lenau, the Merlin figure offered all the qualities inherent in his previously conceived idea of "nature spirits."

The first poem opens with one of Lenau's most arresting stanzas:

Am Kirchhof dort bin ich gestanden,
Wo unten still das Rätsel modert
Und auf den Grabesrosen lodert;
Es blüht die Welt in Todesbanden.
(I, 446)

("I stood in the graveyard where the enigma quietly molders down below and flares up in the fire of grave-roses; the world blossoms in the fetters of death.")

Nature harbors both life and death, and here the poet joins them together in powerful images. He asks nature to forgive him for seeking remedies to cure the sorrows which nature imposed on him as a "harsh blessing." But now, he adds, in the depth of the forest he has torn the "delusive bandages" from his deep wounds. Thus the cycle begins with a dimension not present in the "Schilflieder." Nature is the snythesis of life and death, and the poet must face both aspects of existence. From the poem itself one cannot tell whether or not Lenau was referring to something definite when speaking of "delusive bandages." The nature of the image would point to the personal sphere, for he had used the same expression in a note to Sophie in August, 1837. His works, he wrote, were mere "bloody tatters of an inadequate bandage" (IV, 89). Most likely, the remark in the notes refers to *Savonarola*, his deliberately orthodox Christian poem, to which he was applying the finishing touches at that time (cf. VI, 541). By inference, one could deduce that the respective passage in the "Waldlied" was meant to point to Lenau's attempt to embrace Christianity as a remedy for his mental sufferings. This reasoning would necessitate the introduction of extraneous evidence in the interpretation of the poem—a possible, at times necessary, procedure. But the need for it indicates a flaw in the poem. Lenau did not succeed, in this case, in separating his private from his poetic self.

In the second poem, Lenau illustrates further his attitude to nature and its forces. Here, as in the "Schilflieder," a storm draws up, but it functions merely as a backdrop against which the poet himself is set off. His will power is strengthened in times of external hardships. The storm does not symbolize, as it does in the "Schilflieder," a profound agitation of the domain common to man and nature.

The third poem contains a parallel between teardrops and the first heavy drops of the breaking rainstorm. Only the first stanza depicts the nature scene; the other four elaborate the memory of tears falling from beloved eyes. The last stanza seems to refer to a specific occasion, private in its nature. "The tears welling from her eyes were hot and bitter," the poem ends, "and I shall see these tears roll until I die." The lines refer to a particular instance in the relationship between Lenau and Sophie.

In a way, the fourth poem cancels the effect of the third by assigning a negative significance to it: If you enter the forest "as a stranger," upsetting memories, like robbers, will attack you on its paths. This opening explains the third poem. The poet had entered the forest as a stranger, not giving himself completely to the magic of nature. The breaking thunderstorm he had observed brought up memories that distracted him. The intention expressed at the opening of the cycle—to yield to nature completely—was not realized until now. The fourth poem differs in tone from the earlier ones. Written in iambic trimeter, with feminine endings and numerous enjambements, it moves at a fast pace. The poem is a paean to nature, glorifying its powers of rejuvenation:

Es rauschet wie ein Träumen
Von Liedern in den Bäumen,
Und mit den Wellen ziehen
Verhüllte Melodien.

Im Herzen wird es helle,
Und heim zur ewgen Quelle
Der Jugend darfst du sinken,

Dich frisch und selig trinken.
(I, 449)

("The trees rustle as if dreams of songs went through them, and muted melodies move along with the waves. Your heart turns bright, and you may return to the eternal spring of youth and drink newness and bliss.")

No longer is there the duality of nature and man. The joining of the two is portrayed in images borrowed from Hegel who, in his *Lectures on Nature Philosophy*, wrote of a marriage between nature and mind (*Geist*). The mind, Hegel said in his elusive prose, finds its own counterpart in nature. The study of nature is a way for the spirit to liberate itself in and through nature, but it is the freeing of nature as well. Nature is essentially identical with matters of the mind, but only the mind makes it possible for these matters to realize their existence. The mind, when facing nature, experiences the same inevitability of choice that Adam felt when he first saw Eve: "This is flesh of my flesh; this is bone of my bones. Thus nature is the bride to whom the mind is wed."[12] The image recurs in Lenau's poem:

Sehnsüchtig zieht entgegen
Natur auf allen Wegen,
Als schöne Braut im Schleier,
Dem Geiste, ihrem Freier.
(I, 449)

("Yearningly nature, as a beautiful bride in a veil, sets out to meet the mind, her wooer.")

In the following, Lenau went a step beyond Hegel by showing the "bride" imbued with a yearning for love as well as death. She trembles in anticipation of the "kiss of death." In the last stanza, this image is transferred to the soul of man, which yearns to be wed to God (not the Christian God, certainly, but a general supreme power) and can already feel the breath in which it will perish. The paradox inherent in this poem is characteristic of Lenau. On the one hand, the union with nature is seen as a source of rejuvenation; on the other, it opens a haven that spells oblivion.

The fifth poem is about Merlin. Its form is most unusual for Lenau. Here is one of the few instances where he tore himself away from the strict metric form which elsewhere he observed so closely. There are eight stanzas of varying length —from four to twenty lines—and varying meters. In the first stanza, the three central lines bear three stresses each, the first and seventh lines have two, the second and eighth have four. The rhyme scheme is a a b c c d d b:

Wie Merlin
Möcht ich durch die Wälder ziehn;
Was die Stürme wehen,
Was die Donner rollen
Und die Blitze wollen,
Was die Bäume sprechen,
Wenn sie brechen,
Möcht ich wie Merlin verstehen.
(I, 450)

("Like Merlin, I would like to wander through the forests; like Merlin, I would like to understand what the storms blow, what the thunders call, what the flashes of lightning seek, what the trees are speaking as they break.")

The other stanzas are constructed more regularly. Merlin is completely one with nature. He absorbs and relives it in all its aspects, physically as well as spiritually. He lets lightning cleanse his body and, like the mythical woman-figure in the "Schilflieder," lets his long hair fly in the wind: "Flattern läßt sein Haar Merlin / In der Sturmnacht her und hin" ("Merlin lets his hair fly to and fro in the stormy night."). Nature fills his heart, while lightning kisses his hair. He partakes in the violent as well as in the peaceful manifestations of nature. In a gentle night in spring, with no breeze to move the leaves on the trees, Merlin spins nets of thought between the branches of tall oaks. Through a magic horn held to his ear by the queen of the elves, he hears voices no one else can hear, the "ultra-audible," the fluids of life rushing through trees, and the dreams of birds:

Lauschend hört Merlin entzückt
Unter ihrem Brustgefieder
Träumen ihre künftgen Lieder.
Klingend strömt des Mondes Licht
Auf die Eich und Hagerose,
Und im Kelch der feinsten Moose
Tönt das ewige Gedicht.
(I, 452)

("Transported, Merlin hears under the soft down of the birds' breasts the dreams of their future songs. Melodiously the light of the moon pours upon oak and hedgerose, and the eternal poem resounds in the calyces[13] of the finest moss.")

In the "Schilflieder" the poet himself had been what Merlin is here. He had heard, and given voice to, the secret voices of nature. Eleven years later in the "Waldlieder," Merlin, the incarnation of the "nature spirits," became an image of envy and yearning. He would like to be Merlin; he would try to understand the voices of the forest. The nature spirit is no longer identical with the creative impulse within the poet, but is the object of a nostalgic description. Nature and spirit are united, but the poet can speak of their union only as an outsider. Merlin is gifted with magically heightened perceptions. The voices he hears are inaudible to the human ear. They are nature's most delicate manifestations: sap trickling inside trees; future songs in the breasts of young birds; the "sounds" of the moonlight pouring on oaks and wild roses; and, most illusory of all, the sounds emanating from the chalice of moss.

Synesthetic imagery (the sounding moonlight) removes the scene to a realm more sublime, as well as more ephemeral, than reality. Also, it determines the atmosphere for the final blending of nature and art: It is poetry (nature's eternal poem) that emanates from the moss. All sense perceptions have been fused, and nature affects Merlin in one great experience that carries supernatural overtones. The thought that poetry springs from irrational forces rather than from the mind of a consciously creating artist was widely accepted during Romanticism. It explains the Romanticists' veneration for all kinds of anonymous art, such as folksongs and fairytales. They were believed to be direct outpourings from a subconscious level of creativity, products of the collective genius of a nation or race. To consider nature as a creator of art is merely a further step in the acceptance of a subconscious creativity since, according to Schelling's philosophy, nature is a less developed stage of the spirit of man. Modern psychology has accepted the Romantic tenets of artistic creativity to a large extent. Jung's theories of the collective unconscious as the creator of archetypes are close to the beliefs of the Romanticists.

The "eternal poem" that Merlin hears in nature is more than his sensitive interpretation of sounds which, in reality, cannot be heard and more than the sublime view of a form of poetry which does not exist. The "eternal poem" and the inaudible sounds in nature form a symbolic union and are part of a domain where nature and art (and its creator, man) are the same. Lenau's fifth "Waldlied" is not the eternal poem Merlin hears; it merely speaks of the existence of that poem. It is not like Beethoven's music, characterized by Lenau as tunes which the nature spirits whispered into the first dreams of a beautiful child ("Beethovens Büste" [I, 414]). And yet Lenau's description of the eternal poem, his rendition of the supernatural in nature, emulates that which it renders. In his desire to identify himself with Merlin, the poet gave his lines symbolic proportions. The poem is not a symbol of identity with nature, but of a yearning for this identity.

The sixth poem is short, conventional in form—four four-line stanzas of cross-rhymed iambic-anapaestic trimeters—and simple in diction. The cessation of all movement and life in nature is its subject matter. It is night, and the wind has died down. The birds sit on tree branches, dreaming. Only the murmur of a distant spring can be heard. In this silence, memories take shape quietly. They do not linger, however, but "weep past distantly" (weinen fern vorbei). The strangeness of the diction is significant. The concept of "past," coupled with verbs of motion, is one of the basic patterns in Lenau's imagination. In the present case, the stem of the verb (weep) does not imply motion, and yet it is connected with a prefix suggesting such motion. The result is a compound verb that has no factual meaning, but conveys a strong poetic effect. Permanence was, to Lenau, a foreign concept. Life, happiness, and even pain passed on relentlessly and could not be arrested. The evanescence of things was more significant to him than the things themselves. Whereas the fifth poem concentrated on the yearning for a union with nature and on the creative powers of this union, the sixth conveys resignation to reality. Even memories, insubstantial as they are, merely pass by. The last stanza introduces another compound with the concept of "past," even more unusual than the preceding:

> Daß alles vorübersterbe,
> Ist alt und allbekannt;
> Doch diese Wehmut, die herbe,
> Hat niemand noch gebannt.
>
> (I, 453)

("It is an old and well-known fact that everything dies away; but no one yet has banished [or: arrested] this bitter sadness.")

The compound is *vorübersterben*, literally "to die past." The word *gebannt* in the last line functions as an antithesis to the concept *vorüber,* but it is ambiguous in its actual meaning. It has connotations of "stopped," "banished," but also "held spellbound" and "fixed." Thus the ideas of stanching the flow of time, of banishing sorrows, and of perpetuating emotions through a poem are blended into one poetic image.

The seventh poem presents a form in striking contrast with the sixth. It consists of 43 lines in trochaic pentameter with breaks—one cannot very well speak of stanzas—after the twenty-first, thirty-fifth, and fortieth lines. Each line contains one dactyl, except for lines twenty-five and forty-three, which have two dactyls each. The first lines of the poem further develop the theme of stillness in nature. The quiet is complete now. Even the water of the spring has ceased to murmur. Nature is shown dormant: The leaves "hang sleepily," and a bee has fallen asleep in the "lap of a flower." This atmosphere is then transferred to the poet. He wishes that sleep would descend on him. To him, sleep is more than a redeemer from the harshness of reality; it is a state of creative introspection, a condition that can transform the poet into a Merlin figure. Sleep, he wrote, will steal from him the key to his treasure chamber and take away the weapons of anger, "so that the soul, forgetting all external things, may remember the way to its own depths" (Daß die Seele, rings nach außen vergessend, / Sich in ihre Tiefen hinein erinnre). Sleep appears as the "God of childhood," a "rejuvenator of the world," and a "redeemer of the heart." During daylight, the heart is guarded and inaccessible to life's gentler spirits. Before the heart walk our thoughts heavily armed like lictors, driving away sweet enchantment.

> Aber in der Stille der Nacht, des Schlummers,
> Wacht die Seele heimlich und lauscht wie Hero,
> Bis verborgen ihr Gott ihr naht, herüber
> Schwimmend durch das wallende Meer der Träume.
> (I, 454)

("But in the stillness of night and slumber, the soul wakes secretly and listens like Hero, until her god approaches quietly, swimming through the rolling sea of dreams.")

Like Novalis, who referred to sleep as a "quiet messenger of infinite secrets" (in the second "Hymn to the Night"), Lenau pictures sleep as a key to depths to which consciousness has no access. But whereas the early Romanticist Novalis saw in sleep and night an all-embracing symbol of man's eternal life, of love and death, a "key to the abodes of bliss and death," the late Romanticist Lenau saw in it an entrance to realms within one's self, realms that are not accessible in full consciousness. Night and sleep had a metaphysical and religious value for the early Romanticists; for their successors it had an introspective, psychological interest that is well on the way to systematic psychoanalysis. In trying to tap the subliminal productive unconscious, Lenau anticipated elements of Jung's teaching, and in juxtaposing the intellect and the soul as inimical forces, he greatly influenced the philosopher Ludwig Klages, who referred to Lenau's work as an illustration of his theories in his *The Mind as the Opponent of the Soul* (1932).

Like Merlin in the fifth poem, the poet can hear voices of nature:

> Eine Flöte klang mir im Schlaf zuweilen,
> Wie ein Gesang der Urwelt, Sehnsucht weckend,
> Daß ich süß erschüttert erwacht' in Tränen
> Und noch lange hörte den Ruf der Heimat;
> Bliebe davon ein Hauch in meinen Liedern!
>
> Schlaf, melodischer Freund, woher die Flöte?
> Ist sie ein Ast des Walds, durchhaucht vom Gotte,
> Hört ich im Traum des heiligen Pan Syringe?
> (I, 454)

("A flute sounded through my slumber, now and then, like tunes from a primeval world, giving rise to a yearning in me, so that I awoke in tears, in sweet agitation, and could hear for a long time the call of the homeland; I would that a breath of it were retained in my verses! Sleep, melodious friend, whence came the flute? Is it a branch of the forest, made vocal by the god's breath? Did I hear in my dreams the syrinx of divine Pan?")

The flute is, for Lenau, the voice audible only to the subconscious. Its tunes seem to emanate from a primordial world. They give rise to a yearning for something vaguely remembered. The "homeland" from which they come is a spiritual realm, where the subconscious presses to the surface, where a fulfillment, first vaguely divined in dreams, becomes real. It is a realm mysteriously associated with man's state before birth and after death. The voices which the poet hears in his sleep come from that domain, but he leaves open the question whether or not he will be able to capture a breath of these voices in his poems. As in the fifth poem, the poet is full of yearning for a union with nature, and the voice he gave to this yearning is an achievement in its own right. Novalis, too, in the fourth "Hymn to the Night," spoke of a "homeland" from which light and day are remote. But Novalis' symbol included night, love, and God as the goal of our lives, while Lenau, in his "homeland" image, conjured up a world of primordial unity long lost to a desperate, spiritually unsheltered generation and never to be regained.

Lenau's description of the primordial voices and their origin might be interpreted as a characterization of poetic symbols: They are archetypal images that sound a chord present in every man and they give rise to a feeling of cognition of something that defies rational analysis. In the last three lines, the poet asks about the origin of the sounds he has heard, but his answer is another question. Is the flute a branch breathed upon by a god; is it Pan's syrinx?

In the last two poems of the cycle, Lenau breaks away from the rhapsodic style of the seventh and returns to his accustomed rhymed four-line stanzas. The eighth poem deals with spring, but it is the most melancholy spring poem Lenau ever wrote. It is evening, and the birds drink at a brook before going to rest in the thicket. The poet yearns for a fate similar to that of the birds. He would like to depart, like birds after a spring day, sweetly satisfied and without a complaint. Yet there is in him one last, burning desire: to kneel at the spring of love and drink the happiness for which his soul has been craving, as the birds drink from a brook before nightfall. Aspects from Lenau's personal life enter the poem at this point: his desire for fulfillment of love, for example. Yet the craving for fulfillment is not the foremost thought in the poet's mind. More than with love, he is occupied with his own death, that languid vanishing that he dreamed of toward the end of his life.

In the last poem, Lenau rounds out the cycle by depicting images of the resignation and death of which he spoke in the preceding poem:

Rings ein Verstummen, ein Entfärben;
Wie sanft den Wald die Lüfte streicheln,
Sein welkes Laub ihm abzuschmeicheln;
Ich liebe dieses milde Sterben.

Von hinnen geht die stille Reise,
Die Zeit der Liebe ist verklungen,

Die Vögel haben ausgesungen,
Und dürre Blätter sinken leise.

(I, 455)

("Roundabout, a growing silence and a fading of colors; how softly the winds stroke the forest, caressing it to make it drop its withered leaves; I love this gentle dying. I am silently leaving this place; the time of love has gone, the birds have finished their songs, and dry leaves fall softly.")

Love may not have found fulfillment, but its time has ended like the birds' song. Death comes gently and is welcome. The poem is striking through its unity of atmosphere, language, and movement. Individual expressions connote withdrawal and cessation: *Verstummen, Entfärben, verklingen, von hinnen, nicht mehr, sinken, fallen.*

In the end, everything dies away peacefully—love, nature, the poet's art, and the poet himself. And yet, as an expression of ubiquitous transciency, the poem is most convincing. It offers symbols of sweet decay and lulling death, created by the weary, gravely ill poet who felt the ground slipping from under his feet. The "Waldlieder" may not be as accomplished as the earlier "Schilflieder," but they are greater in scope. They are Lenau's final effort to transmit through poetry his deeply felt doubts about his art, and his resignation to his own fate.

CHAPTER 4

Themes, Topics, and Traditions

I *The Romantic Heritage*

THE themes and topics of Lenau's poetry cover a limited range. The tradition in which his art was rooted—not counting his early effort in the style of the *Hainbund* poets—was that of Romanticism, and many of his motifs are essentially Romantic. The one poem for which Lenau is remembered most frequently, one that every school child knows by heart, is "Der Postillion," beginning:

Lieblich war die Maiennacht,
Silberwölklein flogen,
Ob der holden Frühlingspracht
Freudig hingezogen.
(I, 105)

("Lovely was the night in May; silver clouds were flying, gaily sailing above the sweet splendor of spring.")

A Romantic poem par excellence, "Der Postillion" tells of a night journey by post chaise, with a postilion cracking his whip and blowing his bugle. The rhythm of the verses imitates the gait of the trotting horses. Contrasted with the hurrying carriage and the watchful driver is the peace of the dormant landscape. A journey to far-away places, a postilion and the sound of his horn, a nocturnal nature scene characterized in general terms rather than in descriptive detail—these are the motifs used also in conjuring up the atmosphere in the most romantic of all prose works of Romanticism: Eichendorff's *Aus dem Leben eines Taugenichts*. The journey of Lenau's postilion is interrupted. He stops by a churchyard and tells of his friend who is buried there:

Ein gar herzlieber Gesell!
Herr, 's ist ewig schade!
Keiner blies das Horn so hell
Wie mein Kamerade!

("What a kind and dear fellow he was, sir. It's a shame he had to die. No one could blow a horn so gaily as my dead comrade.")

It is his custom, the postilion says, to stop near his friend's grave and play for him his favorite tune. As he plays on his bugle, the sounds echo in the mountains, and it seems as if the dead friend were returning the salute. The journey continues, but the traveler, who is passive throughout the procedure, has the final lines: "Lang mir noch im Ohre lag / Jener Klang vom Hügel" ("For a long time I imagined I heard that sound from the hill.") The magic of the *Posthorn,* like other Romantic motifs, exerted its spell on Lenau. Yet his use of the motif differs from that of the earlier Romanticists. To them, the sound of the *Posthorn* signified a strong, but hopeful sense of longing, be it homesickness (*Heimweh*), or its opposite (*Fernweh*), a longing for distant places. In another Lenau poem, "Das Posthorn," the bugle sounds exclusion and bitter solitude. The poet, awake and contending with his pain, is reminded of men's quick readiness to leave one another. "Didn't somebody stand by the door of the carriage, with tears in his eyes?" he asks, and continues:

Mag er stehn! die Träne kann
Nicht die Rosse halten;
Mag der rauhe Geißelschwung
Ihm die Seele spalten!

(I, 14)

("Let him stand there! His tears cannot hold back the horses; may the harsh crack of the whip split his soul in two!")

The poem ends with a reminder of death and the grave awaiting the poet.

Grave and churchyard, too, are motifs that Lenau shared with the earlier Romanticists. To them, the churchyard was a place of introspection, of a magically heightened sensitivity, and a realm related to the hereafter. It was at the grave of his beloved that Novalis, in his *Hymns to the Night,* experienced the vision of an open heaven and of his beloved appearing between the clouds, leading him into a "new life." Lenau's churchyards convey no transcendental symbolism. They spell desolation. It is a fact that Lenau grew up among graves. In 1817 and after, Mrs. Vogel and her children lived in Ofen in a superficially converted chapel in the middle of an old graveyard.[1] In the poem "Vergänglichkeit" (I, 118), gravestones function as permanent signals of grief and are contrasted with man's heart where sorrow for the dead has no permanent place. Transiency, the destroyer of childhood and love, puts an end to man's mourning as well. Leaning crosses on gravemounds transmit a drowsiness that pervades nature in "Die Wurmlinger Kapelle" (I, 51). The graveyard is part of the alluring, sweet *Todesmüdigkeit* (lethal fatigue), a weariness unto death that has seized the poet's heart. Unlike Novalis, Lenau could not consider the place of death a stepping stone to more sublime realms. It did not grant him a glimpse into a blissful hereafter, but it impressed itself upon him as an absolute end.

In the sonnet "Der Seelenkranke," fatigue and the death-wish acquire pathological connotations. The poet suffers from a wound in his heart. He feels it sapping his life and gnawing into him ever more deeply. The only person in whom he could confide, his mother, lies buried. He appeals to her to help him and tend to his needs:

So lass mich bald aus diesem Leben scheiden,
Ich sehne mich nach einer stillen Nacht,
O hilf dem Schmerz, dein müdes Kind entkleiden.
(I, 300)

("Let me soon depart from this life. I yearn for a quiet night. Oh help pain to put your weary child to bed.")

In his pain and helplessness, the poet lets his imagination reduce him to the state of a child. He sees himself as being sick and in his mother's care, a childhood recollection that assumes archetypal significance in this context. Undressing a child and getting him ready for bed are gestures of motherly love and care and convey the feeling of utmost comfort. But here the mother is dead, and the loving help her child begs for would mean a gentle easing into the hereafter. Fatigue, in this poem, is conveyed in deeply experienced, archetypal images.

Among the motifs of Romanticism that also appear in Lenau's poems are childhood and dreams, friendship and the pangs of separation, ruins of old castles, chapels, and the ubiquitous rose.[2] Lenau's fascination with nature, his tendency to project human characteristics into it, betrays the Romantic heritage. The beauty of the mountains was a favorite subject matter for many Romantic poets, as it was for Goethe. Lenau's particular predilection for the Austrian Alps bespeaks a certain sense of realism that sets him apart from the earlier Romanticists who were usually not concerned with the geographic location of their settings. Lenau wrote poems about definite places in the

Alps, for example "Der schwarze See" (I, 347) and "Der Laudachsee" (I, 486).[3] As a young man, he was an enthusiastic if only occasional mountain climber, a not too common pastime in his days.

Lenau was one of the first German poets to write poems about the ocean. Although Goethe and Schiller, among others, had written occasional verses dealing with the sea, few poets had seen and experienced what they were writing about. Yet, despite Lenau's close acquaintance with the sea, he treated it in very general terms in his poems. He was not concerned with it for its own sake, but made it function as a medium of ideas and emotions. A group of poems entitled "Atlantica" is a case in point. In one of the poems, "Meeresstille" (I, 147), the calm of the sea suggests to the poet a sadness pervading nature and evokes in him the idea that a human race may be living on the bottom of the ocean, listening to nature's woe. Another poem from this group, "Seemorgen" (I, 148), presents a fresh breeze and a fast moving ship. But the joy of experiencing motion is not unmitigated: There is still the endless expanse of water before the poet's eyes, and it stirs within him an impatient yearning for mountains and meadows. A sea voyage means leaving one's homeland behind ("An mein Vaterland" [I, 149]), or it may be a panacea after a heartbreaking experience ("Wandel der Sehnsucht" [I, 22]).

Again, no consistent pattern evolves in Lenau's use of a given image. The only unifying aspect of all the occurrences of the sea is the general function Lenau assigned to it: The sea is not an entity in itself, a piece of reality that can exercise poetic force when described by a poet; but it gains reality only as a background for human affairs, or, at best, as an agent interfering with man on human terms. The only exception to this is "Sturmesmythe," discussed in Chapter 3. In Lenau's other sea poems—and there are a fair number of them—the sea motif is not given poetic dimensions.

II *America*

Lenau's stay in America, disappointing though it was to him, nevertheless bore some poetic fruit. The German reading public was very receptive to literary accounts of America; nowhere else in Europe, in fact, was the interest in the new continent as great as it was in Germany. Between the years 1815 and 1850, more than fifty books on travel in America were brought out by

German publishers.[4] An important factor was the return of some 17,000 German mercenaries—soldiers who had fought on both sides during the War of Independence—and the informed first-hand accounts they gave of their adventures. America became a popular theme in German literature, and many poets seriously considered emigration: Maximilian Klinger, Heinrich Leopold Wagner, Wilhelm Heinse, Friedrich Schiller, August Wilhelm Schlegel, August von Platen, and Anastasius Grün. Klinger's play *Sturm und Drang,* which gave its name to a literary movement, is set in America, even though it contains no local color whatsoever.

Lenau was not the first German-speaking poet to set foot on American ground. This honor goes to Johann Gottfried Seume (1763-1810), then a student of theology, who in 1782 was shanghaied by a recruiting officer, impressed into service, sold to the King of England, and shipped to America. He managed to desert the following year and wrote in his autobiography[5] a delightful account of his trip to America, full of enthusiasm for the New World despite the untoward circumstances. Adelbert von Chamisso took part in a scientific expedition around the world in 1815-1818 during which he also visited America. The third German writer was an unruly Austrian priest, Karl Postl. He disappeared mysteriously from Vienna in 1823 and landed in New Orleans in the same year, assuming a new identity and a new name, Charles Sealsfield. Quickly adapting himself to his new home, he launched a remarkable career as a writer, merchant, journalist, farmer, and even political agent. His novels and stories about America and her people are realistic and show his rare gift for close observation.

The attitude of Sealsfield's younger countryman, Lenau, was the exact opposite. The statement is often made that Lenau's views on America were biased, that he never even tried to exercise objectivity in judging all the new impressions, and that he was narrowly selective in recording his transoceanic experiences. This is quite true, but one should, in all fairness, not expect anything else of Lenau. He showed the very same attitude in every aspect of his life and works, and it would indeed have been incongruous if, upon stepping on American soil, he had suddenly changed his character and personality and become the objective recorder of external reality. His impressions of America, as of the sea, were of interest to him only if they struck a related chord within him, if they found their way to the sensitive nerve of his poetic self.

Lenau wrote four of the five poems in the "Atlantica" group while in America (cf. III, 198), but all other poems set in America or dealing with the American experience were written after his return to Europe, and most of them not until 1836. While in America, Lenau wrote mostly poems with a European setting.[6]

Death and transiency, wherever Lenau found them, moved him deeply and stirred his imagination. In "Der Urwald" (I, 268), a long poem in rhymed iambic pentameter, he depicted a decaying forest, relating it to himself and to the waning of his energy and will to live. The primeval forest had been the scene of a battle between life and death, he wrote, a battle that had lasted for millenia. Finally, life was subdued. In vain it keeps trying to sprout forth from the tight fist which death has clenched around it. The poet sees his own life suffocating in the same fist of death and wonders whether or not it would remain closed forever. He compares his life to the forest, which appears withered and drab and abandoned by song birds. His life seems equally stunted, and its song birds, his poems, have vanished. The ancient forest, celebrated by the Romanticists as a symbol of creative virginity and looked forward to by Lenau as a decisive new experience, is reduced, like the ocean, to a two-dimensional correlative of the poet's psychic condition.

On the other hand, considerable local color is provided in "Das Blockhaus" (I, 273), a poem in free verse with varying rhyme schemes. Lenau describes a stay at a small inn during a journey through the "forests of the Republic." The reception by the innkeeper is cool, but not unfriendly. He shakes hands without squeezing the fingers—straightforward and determined not to lie even with his fingertips. The guest feels well and secure after this welcome. The innkeeper takes his time waiting on the table, but the room is warm and the food is good. After everyone has gone to bed, the poet remains alone and immediately turns his back on his present environment. No longer does he think of what he saw and heard, but drinks a bottle of Rhine wine he had brought along in his voluminous luggage and reads a book of Uhland's poetry. The oak logs that burn in the fireplace bring up melancholy thoughts: Perhaps there is no such thing as being alone; perhaps he, the poet, is merely a burning piece of wood, giving off warmth for the benefit of an invisible guest. The idea is startling and near the border of insanity. Again, the question concerning the reality of existence is posed in a context that did not seem to suggest it.

Before leaving for America, Lenau had singled out the virgin forest and Niagara Falls as absolutely necessary experiences for his growth as a poet. His work, he wrote to Schurz from Heidelberg (III, 145f.), was intricately interwoven with nature, and nature in America was more beautiful and unrestrained than in Europe. He expected to come upon a great store of images and impressions, untouched as the floor of the great forests. He hoped that in America a new world of poetry would open up before him and that something within himself, unknown to him, would be awakened by the thundering call of the Niagara. The forests, as his poems show, did not add a new dimension to his poetic vision. Niagara Falls, on the other hand, impressed him deeply. He traveled there in the spring of 1833, shortly before his return to Europe. Three poems result from this experience: "Verschiedene Deutung" (I, 271), "Niagara" (I, 272), and "Die drei Indianer" (I, 112).

The first poem is divided into two parts and conveys two different interpretations of a natural phenomenon. The water of the falls, upon hitting rocks, is turned into thin spray of many colors or even into "wet dust." As so often, Lenau draws a parallel between the natural phenomenon and the realm of man. In the first part of the poem, man is compared to the river. Like the water, he has to be shattered and dispersed if he is to receive light from above. In the second part, each of the tiny particles of spray is considered as a human entity, a "poor self," but all of them together are resplendent in the heavenly harmony of colors. The poem could be discounted as offering another of Lenau's numerous man-nature parallels if it were not for its being based on a genuine and detailed observation of external reality. Lenau's precise record of the play of colors at the bottom of the falls makes the poem noteworthy and shows that a fascinating natural phenomenon could at times absorb the poet's close attention.

The same is true of the second poem, "Niagara." Again a parallel is drawn between nature and man, but a close observation provides the basis for the comparison, which then merely comprises the last two lines of eight stanzas, almost as an afterthought. The phenomenon described is paradoxical in character. The traveler who approaches the falls from Buffalo along the Niagara River will hear the roar of the cataract from a considerable distance. As he gets closer, the river flows faster, gushing over small rapids and causing sufficient noise to drown out the sound of the falls. The closer one gets to the falls, the less audible they become. Lenau described this phenomenon in great detail, in rhythmically powerful lines. When, toward the end of the poem, the water is seen in images of animation, the most deeply engraved pattern in Lenau's thinking becomes apparent, illustrating once more the statement he made about himself in a note to Sophie: "My innermost being is the domain of death" (IV, 189). As the river approaches the precipice, it flows faster, as if drawn by a mysterious force:

Die Stromschnellen stürzen, schießen,
Donnern fort im wilden Drang,
Wie von Sehnsucht hingerissen
Nach dem großen Untergang.
(I, 272)

("The rapids rush, hurl themselves, and thunder away in a wild urge, as if torn along by a yearning for the great destruction.")

The comparison at the end of the poem plays on the symbolic connotations of the great "fall." Transposing the concept of space into one of time, Lenau wrote:

Und so mag vergebens lauschen,
Wer dem Sturze näher geht;
Doch die Zukunft hörte rauschen
In der Ferne der Prophet.
(I, 273)

(" In vain will he listen who approaches the fall [downfall, end] closely; but the prophet could hear the sound of the future in the distance.")

The prophet is one of doom, and the "downfall" he predicts has implications that reach far beyond the falling of water.

At the time of Lenau's visit to Niagara Falls, Indian women of the Chippewa tribe sold souvenirs and other trinkets on Goat Island, located between the two falls.[7] It is likely that Lenau encountered some of these peddlars and was upset by the contrast between his romantic image of the heroic Indian—a concept he shared with most continental Europeans—and the reality he saw:[8] a few subservient paupers intent on finding their place in a culture brought to their shores by mercantile intruders. The decline of the Indian was a theme well established in literature by the time of Lenau's visit. François René de Chateaubriand (1768-1848) was Lenau's most prominent forerunner as a portrayer of the fate of the American Indian. He had traveled in North America—especially in the area surrounding Niagara Falls—in 1791, and had given a moving picture of the Indian in his story *Atala,* published in 1801. His influence on European letters was tremendous. By 1830 the fate of the American Indian was a favorite topic of conversation in the literary salons of Vienna,[9] and Lenau's poems on the Indians can be considered part of a fashion. He could have treated the theme without ever coming to America.

Lenau rejected the depressing bit of reality he had seen at Niagara Falls and, more in step with literary tradition, created a different image of the Indian, that of the noble savage unwilling and unable to submit to a changed world. His poem "Die drei Indianer" combines the motif of Niagara Falls with that of the Indian. In a series of violent images, Lenau describes a storm raging on the banks of the Niagara River. An infuriated sky shatters great oaks, drowns out the voice of the falls, and whips the foaming waves. Three Indians, a father and his two grown sons, stand at the bank, listening to the "death moans" of the forest. The scene is set for the portrayal of a violent death. The old Indian utters scathing curses against the white men, against every wave that carried them to their shores, every breath of wind that served their ships, and every reef that failed to wreck them. The white conquerors, he says, left the Indians with nothing but a deadly hatred. It is significant that Lenau, instead of following up these outbursts of verbal violence with an equally violent aggressive action, merely tells of the Indians' decision to commit suicide. The father announces that he and his sons will die by letting themselves be carried down the cataract in their canoe. With their arms locked, singing a song of death, they throw away their oars and face the approaching falls:

> Laut ununterbrochne Donner krachen,
> Blitze flattern um den Todesnachen,
> Ihn umtaumeln Möwen sturmesmunter;
>
> Und die Männer kommen festentschlossen
> Singend schon dem Falle zugeschossen,
> Stürzen jetzt den Katarakt hinunter.
>
> (I, 113)

("Continuous thunder crashes loudly, lightning flashes about the death boat, and sea gulls flutter around it gaily in the storm: and the singing men, determined, come rushing toward the falls, and are hurled down the cataract.")

The images have archetypal overtones: the number three, a "death boat" crossing the waters to a realm of oblivion, and elements of nature enhancing the scene of destruction.

In a second poem concerning the fate of the Indians, "Der Indianerzug," Lenau applied the same imaginary pattern as in the preceding one: The Indians are forced to give way. In the second poem, the move does not take them toward their death, but merely away from their homeland.

> Wehklage hallt am Susquehannaufer,
> Der Wandrer fühlt sie tief sein Herz durchschneiden;
> Wer sind die lauten, wildbewegten Rufer?
> Indianer sinds, die von der Heimat scheiden.
>
> (I, 108)

("Lamentations resound on the bank of the Susquehanna, touching deeply the wanderer's heart; who are the tumultuous, emotion-torn callers? They are Indians leaving their homeland.")

The chieftain, a white-haired man with burning eyes, steps among his people, denouncing the newcomers and cursing their plows that will tear into the graves of the natives' forefathers. As in the preceding poem, the Indians, although burning with hatred, do not offer any resistance. Like the three going down the cataract, they are caught irresistibly in a current that sweeps them along. "The accursed whites press us ever further, as if we were their cattle, ever further, further" (I, 108). The threefold repetition of "further" (*weiter*) determines the image of motion as the predominant characteristic of the poem. The Indians leave the forest of their "childhood sleep" (*Kindesschlaf*), where they had hunted game, embraced their beloved, and buried their dead. As they pass the graves of their ancestors, the chieftain admonishes his people to tread softly lest they wake them, admitting their shame, which is the recantation of their belief. Still imbued with the same pride and nobility which their forefathers possessed, the outcast Indians no longer have their strength, their energy and courage. The conquerors brought with them the Christian cross, the chieftain exclaims, supposedly as a symbol of salvation. In reality it signified the destruction of the Indians whose courage for revenge has been nailed to the cross. In the end, the fleeing Indians look back at their native soil and see their forests go up in flames, as the new masters go about clearing the land for their agricultural pursuits.

The image of Lenau's Indian coincided with that of most European writers of his day, in broad terms, but it differed in one respect. Other writers portrayed the Indian as quiet, unperturbed, never yielding, and dying heroically, whereas Lenau's Indian bears characteristics of the poet himself. Frustrated and emasculated, he was akin to the generation of poets born into the last phase of the Romantic movement, a generation to whom the verve and enthusiasm of their fathers was something to envy (or to ridicule), but not to live up to. They were the heirs to a culture which they could cope with intellectually, but not emotionally. Introspective, overly sensitive, critical, ironic, sophisticated, and filled with ennui, they lacked the energy of those who could see themselves as initiators of a new cultural era. Lenau's Indian is a projection of the sentiments of a generation into an exotic environment. Faced with the necessity of coping with a hitherto unknown enemy, Lenau's Indian does not stand his ground. He becomes the expatriate, the homeless wanderer, filled with a consuming, yet ineffectual rage against those who superseded him. The image of the three Indians rushing down Niagara Falls in a suicidal ecstasy that carries erotic connotations was to Lenau a projection of a deep yearning within himself. The Indians in the present poem follow more closely the pattern of Lenau's actual inner experiences. Scions of a proud heritage, they are helpless and driven, unable to live and unable to die.

Of all the motifs which the American journey suggested to the poet, that of the Indian was the most fruitful, not because it provided a seed for new poetic ideas, but because it fell into place within the existing realm of his poetic imagination. To be sure, the journey offered to Lenau numerous other motifs, new to him as well as to German literature, but it could not change the focus of his poetic vision.

III *"The Unsheltered"*

The sensation of being without shelter, conveyed here through the figure of the Indian, haunted Lenau continuously. One of the motifs he used to translate it into poetry was the figure of Ahasuerus, the Wandering Jew. To a number of Romantic poets, Ahasuerus had become a symbol of pervading despair, a sensation well conveyed in an image of spatial relations: homelessness and eternal wandering. It would be difficult to imagine a greater contrast in the concept of man than that between the late eighteenth century humanitarian, as exemplified in Lessing's Nathan, this supreme being, tolerant and reconciled to the world, and Lenau's figure of Ahasuerus, a desperate outcast, fierce and unbridled in the expression of his inner torment. Lenau wrote two poems about the Wandering Jew. Both of them center on one aspect of the motif: that the Jew's fate is perpetual and never ending. Ahasuerus is the legendary character who refused to help Christ carry His cross and was condemned to roam the world forever. In both poems, he is juxtaposed with peaceful villagers and hunters and their normal, if difficult, life.

"Ahasver, der ewige Jude" (I, 74) opens with a melancholy nature scene: a desolate stretch of land, a heath unadorned by trees and bushes. In the distance, earth and sky merge along an undefined horizon. A community of shepherds live in the region, in modest, straw-thatched cottages. The reader is told that they had to sustain the blow that is considered the severest in human existence, namely, death of one close to them. A young man has died, and the community is gathered around his bier under a linden tree. At this point, Ahasuerus enters and the described setting, mournful and melancholy as it seemed to be, now turns idyllic by comparison to the aura surrounding the frightful visitor. He approaches as if driven by an invisible force, his white hair flying in the wind. His face, pale and rigid, "juts into the realm of life gravely and forbiddingly, like old, crumbling rock" (I, 75). His burning eyes speak of disgust with the world. Stepping up to the bier, he chides the villagers for lamenting at the sight of death and admonishes them to pray quietly, lest they wake the dead youth. "Could I," he exclaims, "only rest in the arms of eternal sleep, as he does!" A good part of Ahasuerus' lamentations at the bier are about general human concerns as much as they are about the protagonist and his particular fate. The dead youth, he says, was redeemed from this earth before he could awake from the blissful sleep of childhood, before the crude fist of life could reach for his heart and drive away young dreams. The peaceful expression on the dead man's face, Ahasuerus exclaims bitterly, continues to relate the fairy tale that our earth is a paradise. It is significant that the protagonist first contrasts the gentle, short life of the youth with man's fate in general, rather than with himself.

Lenau's primary concern in the Ahasuerus poems was the symbolic transference of the figure of the Wandering Jew to all mankind, and especially to his own generation. Ahasuerus speaks for Lenau when he sneers at the sameness of all experiences, at the repetitiousness of all events, and when he chastises nature for keeping up her endless cycle of budding and wilting. Life is compared to a gypsy woman prophesying the future in a deck of cards. She shuffles them and arranges them in what appears to be a new order, but the patterns that emerge are ever the same. Ahasuerus has spent eighteen hundred years observing the game and has long ago despaired of encountering a variation. His one and only desire is denied to him: death. He has embraced fire and water, but to no avail. Fire withdrew from him, and the waves tossed him back to the shore. When he hurled himself from a mountain top, his body defied the law of gravity. Poison and diseases could do him no harm. In the end, Ahasuerus takes leave, resuming his eternal journey.

By fusing the concepts of ennui, of a pervading disgust with life, with the image of the Wandering Jew, Lenau gave them a striking aspect of timelessness. Ahasuerus became not only a poetic vehicle transmitting Lenau's own despair, but a figure of archetypal significance. He is an enhancement of the attitude toward life of an entire generation, transporting it into the domain of ageless symbols.[10]

In Lenau's other Ahasuerus poem, "Der ewige Jude" (I, 228), the protagonist appears only in a daydream of the poet. While travelling in the mountains, he rests at the cottage of a poacher. After a hearty meal, in an attempt to entertain the stranger, the poacher's wife proudly shows him her possessions,—little trinkets, rings, necklaces, and coins. One coin catches the poet's eye. It is made of a crude lead and depicts Christ as He collapses under the burden of the cross. In a daydream, comprising almost half of the forty-six-stanza poem, the poet imagines a scene that explains to him the origin of the coin.

While pursuing mountain goats over barren rock, a hunter encounters a gigantic, fearsome old man who threatens to kill him unless the hunter shoots a bullet at the man's heart:

> "Schieß her!" ruft sein toddürstendes Gebrülle,
> "Sonst stirb!" ruft sein todlechzendes Geheule.
> (I, 233)

("'Shoot at me!' sound his death-thirsty roars, 'or die!' sound his death-yearning howls.")

Trembling, the hunter complies, but the lead bullet bounces off Ahasuerus' body as if it had hit a rock. No form of death is accessible to him, neither the violent nor the gentle. "Could I but die away in the mountains like my own lamentations," he exclaims, while trudging on. He sees himself as something inconsequential and immaterial, which nevertheless is cursed with perpetuity—a shadow that outlasts the object by which it is cast, an echo nailed to the face of a mountain, a blade of grass eternally resisting hail, and an ephemeral ray of light walled up in rock. These images are striking in their paradoxical quality and come from subtle layers of Lenau's inner experiences. When, in the end, the poacher picks up the bullet that failed to penetrate Ahasuerus' heart, he finds it flattened into a coin, portraying the torment that besets the Wandering Jew's heart.

There is a third occurrence of the Ahasuerus motif in Lenau's work: the Jew Tubal in *Savonarola,* who is a mirror image of the Ahasuerus figure, except that he dies, reconciled with God and having become a Christian. Fate had imbued him with a boundless hatred. His three sons had been taken from him and killed, and their blood was used for a transfusion to aid the ailing Pope. Tubal, demented and in flight from an asylum, wanders through the city of Rome aimlessly, shouting his hatred against the Pope and Christendom. Later, after having witnessed the martyrdom of Savonarola, he undergoes a change of heart and dies peacefully under an image of the cross. This solution, so uncharacteristic of Lenau, is in keeping with the spirit of the poem in which it occurs.

III *Gypsies and Poles*

The Wandering Jew and the Indian represent a larger group of recurrent characters in Lenau's work: the social outcast. The poet projected the deeply experienced sensation of being without shelter—in the physical as well as in the metaphysical sense—into a number of figures of symbolic significance.

One type of social outcast that Lenau treated repeatedly was the gypsy. In Lenau's works, he is part of the Hungarian landscape, of the area where Lenau grew up. In the first half of the nineteenth century, Hungary was a relatively new and exotic motif in German literature. Three German writers before Lenau had traveled in Hungary: Friedrich Nicolai (1733-1811), Lessing's early friend; Ernest Moritz Arndt (1769-1860); and Friedrich Schlegel (1772-1829). The Romanticists, in general, were fascinated by Hungarian history, language, literature, and folklore. A number of anthologies and collections of Hungarian fairy tales, legends, plays, and stories appeared in German translation.[11] Friedrich Schlegel's lectures on literature at the University of Vienna in 1812 included influential, if fanciful, remarks on Hungarian literature and history. Yet Hungary, unlike Italy and Western Europe, was not exploited for literary motifs by the Romantic poets, with the exception of Clemens Brentano's frolicking story "Die mehreren Wehmüller und ungarischen Nationalgesichter" ("The Several Messrs. Wehmüller and the Hungarian National Faces," 1817) which takes place in Hungary, is rich in local color, and teems with fiddling gypsies, Latin-speaking Hussars, dancing peasants, witches, and black cats. Two plays, Theodor Körner's *Zriny* (1812) and Franz Grillparzer's *Ein treuer Diener seines Herrn* (1828) deal with incidents in Hungarian history; but these are isolated cases.

Lenau was the first major German or Austrian poet to write about Hungary with authority and from a close personal acquaintance. He had spent his entire youth there, spoke Hungarian well enough to converse with natives, and, when in trouble with the Austrian bureau of censorship in 1837, he maintained that he, a Hungarian national, would have nothing to do with Austrian authorities. (His plea was rejected on the ground that he had used Austrian passports for years.) At times Lenau is even referred to as a "Hungarian poet," but such epithets should be used with extreme caution. It is correct if used in the sense of the first half of the nineteenth century, when it had no nationalistic connotations, but simply meant "from the area known as Hungary." But if used in the present-day sense, such attributes are no longer valid. To us, a "Hungarian poet" would be a poet who writes in Hungarian and identifies himself with the Hungarian nation as an ethnic group. This is definitely not true for Lenau, any more than for his famous "Hungarian" contemporary, the composer Franz Liszt. When some literary scholars refer to Lenau as a Hungarian, they have the support of Lenau himself who, like Liszt, called himself one, and yet they are correct only in an outdated specialized sense.

Lenau had deeply experienced the beauty of the Hungarian landscape and the atmosphere of Hungarian life. To be sure, his view was a predominantly Romantic one and presented those aspects of Hungarian life that have subsequently found their way into many an operetta by Johann Strauss and Franz Lehar, aspects which the modern Hungarian loathes as vehemently as the modern German dislikes his national image as it is presented in, say, *The Student Prince*. But it is true that Lenau's poems convey the atmosphere of rural Romantic Hungary so perfectly that to this day many Germans cannot think of Hungary without thinking of Lenau's poems, and vice versa.

Lenau's poems with Hungarian motifs have a strong musical quality and are free, to a great extent, of the melancholy that is characteristic of his other poetry. The gypsy, the particular form of the social outcast in these poems, is a gaily conceived, almost enviable character. It is significant that Lenau never returned to Hungary as a grown man. The happy, romanticized Hungarian setting was to him, poignantly, a childhood recollection. But it was genuine, and the poet had the gift to make a time lost and bygone come to life again in his works. "Die drei Zigeuner" (I, 259) depicts three contented social outcasts, resting under a tree. One plays the fiddle, one watches the smoke rise from his pipe, the third sleeps. They are in rags, but they need no worldly goods to be happy. The poet gratefully acknowledges the lesson they taught him: When life shows itself to us at its worst, one can fiddle it away, smoke it away, sleep it away, and disdain it. "Die Heideschenke" (I, 69) offers considerably more local color. Travelling through Hungary, the poet encounters a herd of horses, driven at breakneck speed by stablehands. This initial scene sets a pattern of fast motion for the entire poem. The narrator hears gypsy music from within a tavern and enters. Young couples dance, but the men turn out to be robbers—next to gypsies, the most popular inhabitants of the Hungarian steppes. Their leader does not join the dance but watches over it. At one point, he goes outside and puts his ear to the ground. He hears what he expected to hear: Hussars approaching, out to capture his band. He shouts at the dancers through the open door, and his voice is so powerful that it drowns out the music. At lightning speed, the tavern empties:

> Und eh das Herz mir dreimal schlug,
> So saßen sie zu Pferde,
> Und auf und davon im schnellen Flug,
> Daß rings erbebte die Erde.
>
> (I, 73)

("Before my heart beat three times, they were astride their horses. Off they were in fast flight, making the earth tremble.")

The poem, simple and unpretentious as it is, shows a perfect blending of rhythmic motion, imagery, color, and light. Its ebullience is genuine, and its powerful verse rings true.

The figure of the bandit gave Lenau the opportunity to portray a type fascinating and enviable to him: that of the outcast who does not suffer passively but takes revenge against society in an energetic, predatory way. His thinking is practical, his emotions suppressed or nonexistent. The character of Görg in *Faust,* although he is not a bandit, shows the same practical, almost nihilistic attitude. Lenau's bandits go about their business efficiently and sometimes even with a sense of humor—a sentiment otherwise absent in Lenau's work. The protagonist in "Der Räuber im Bakony" (I, 223) is a swineherd who pursues his shady affairs on the side, while his charges roam through the woods in search of food. The swineherd, axe in hand, stands under a tree and waits. If he is out to kill a pig, he hurls the axe and never misses. If a traveller happens by, he proceeds similarly. The poem is interesting for a specific reason. Its possible source is a Hungarian folksong and bagpipe tune, "Itthon van-e a kanász" ("Is the Swineherd at Home?" [cf. VI, 304]), one of the very few instances where a piece of Hungarian literature may be reflected in a poem by Lenau. In the folksong, the swineherd is not necessarily a bandit (although very handy with the axe), but the potential evildoer is the narrator. He desires the swineherd's pretty wife and contemplates roasting the husband. At the fire, he could keep warm and smoke his pipe.

In a number of poems with a Hungarian setting, the musical quality that is always present in Lenau's work is underscored thematically. Lenau was fond of gypsy music and spoke about it in some of his poems, making its sweet and wild qualities come to life in words. "Die Werbung" (I, 156) describes the successful efforts of a recruiting officer and his team to enlist a young man in the cavalry. The situation did not spring from Lenau's imagination. He merely described a scene that was common in Hungary, especially in the eighteenth century, but also as late as the war against Prussia in 1866.

The recruitment of soldiers in Hungary was then a particular ritual, and Lenau presented it successfully in his poem. The recruiting team included a gypsy band—a bassviol, flutes or clarinets, violins, and the ever-present cimbalon (a large dulcimer)—and a dozen hussars, accoutered in spurs and sabre, who arrange themselves in a circle and performed a rhythmic dance. The music played was a genre of its own, the so-called "verbunko" (from the German "Werbung," meaning "recruitment"), and consisted of a slow and a fast part, called "lassu" and "friska." As the dance progresses, the soldiers, led by their recruiting officer (always a sergeant), invite eligible young men among the onlookers to join them in the circle. If one does accept, his cap is quickly exchanged for a shako, and the deal is sealed with a toast from a mysteriously produced bottle of wine and a handshake with the recruiting officer. If a potential joiner is reluctant to enter the circle, the team employs methods of gentle persuasion, chiding him and facetiously questioning his courage and manhood.

Lenau used most of these factual details in his poem, while imitating the pounding trochaic rhythm of the music:

> Lauter immer, immer toller
> Braust der Instrumente Kampf,
> Braust die alte Heldenweise,
> Die vor Zeiten wohl mit Macht
> Frische Knaben, welke Greise
> Hinzog in die Türkenschlacht.
> (I, 156)

("Ever more loudly and wildly booms the contest of instruments, booms the old heroic tune which in bygone times pulled young boys and old men into battle against the Turks.")

The recruiting officer has his eye on one particular young man who seems torn between a yearning for the adventurous life of a soldier and the wish to return to his mother and his girl. Suddenly, a sinister figure appears inside the circle and whispers something in the officer's ear, causing him to double his efforts. Then the figure proceeds to the band, inciting them with softly spoken words and myterious glances. The music grows even more intense and irresistible:

> Aus des Basses Sturmgewittern,
> Mit unendlich süßem Sehnen,
> Mit der Stimmen weichem Zittern,
> Singen Geigen, Grabsirenen.
> (I, 158)

("Out of the rumbling thunder of the bass, with infinitely sweet yearning, with softly trembling voices, sing the violins, sirens from the realm of death.")

Before the mysterious stranger leaves—the poet does not say who he is, but refers to him as a "demon"—he arrests the youth's eye with a piercing look. The young man's resistance breaks down, and he steps forward. Some of the onlookers have tears in their eyes, and the poem ends with a question: Is it because the spectators comprehend the dilemma of honor, or because they are thinking of the youth's early grave?

"Die Werbung" is an early poem, written perhaps in 1826 or 1827. It made a great impression on the Swabian Poets and gave Lenau an exotic aura in their eyes. The recollection of the recruitments which he had personally observed in Hungary, and of the music that accompanied them, must have remained with Lenau throughout his life. An accomplished musician and violinist of high order, he often entertained his friends with recitals on his precious Guarnerius, and Hungarian music was his favorite choice.

The lyric-epic cycle "Mischka" (see Chapter 5) is concerned with the magic power of a gypsy virtuoso, and the same theme recurs twice in *Faust,* in the scenes "Der Tanz" and "Görg." In the first, the violin playing of Mephistopheles, the gypsy virtuoso par excellence, serves an erotic function and helps Faust seduce a country girl. The passage consists of fast moving anapests and is extremely lush and sensuous in tone (II, 31-32). In the scene "Görg," the sailors of a wrecked ship dance with girls in a tavern on the seacoast to what appears to be, somewhat incongruously, gypsy music.

Besides music, dance, and the gypsy, there are other aspects of Lenau's Hungarian experiences that emerge from his poems. The most prominent is the image of the heath, the Hungarian steppe. More than the exuberant recollection of gypsy music, the image of the heath—desolate plains with modest vegetation—could be absorbed into the poet's later concept of a gloomy and barren nature. The heath is the dominant image in five poems arranged under the title "Heidebilder" (I, 64), including "Himmelstrauer," "Robert und der Invalide," and "Die Heideschenke." The heath is the proper setting for man in his solitude ("Einsamkeit" [I, 304]), a place forsaken by the "joys and embellishments of life" ("Zweifel und Ruhe" [I, 219]).

Lenau's frequent use of still, dark ponds, fringed by pale rushes, reflects another lasting recollection from Hungary. His bodies of water are rarely of the Alpine variety, clear and surrounded by green hills. They are reminiscent of the shallow, murky ponds in the Eastern part of Austria and Hungary, such as Lake Neusiedel, which Lenau must have passed many times during his travels between Vienna, Pressburg, and Ungarisch-Altenburg. The setting of his "Schilflieder" (I, 18), with their willows and rushes, their pond and water-fowl, resembles Lake Neusiedel or any other similar body of water in that region.

Another recurrent figure signifying homelessness in Lenau's poems is that of the heroic Pole. Following the suppression of the Polish uprising against Russia in 1830, a great number of Polish exiles poured into central Europe. Their fate soon became a favorite literary subject matter, for it offered two motifs dear to the hearts of the late Romantic generation. The exiled Pole could be seen as a political figure on the one hand, and as a symbol of homelessness on the other. In German literature, heroic treatments of the Pole were so numerous that the theme was eventually parodied in poems by Heine and in a *Novelle* by Gottfried Keller, *Kleider machen Leute*. To Lenau, the figure of the homeless Pole was still a serious matter. He found his friends in Stuttgart full of enthusiasm for the cause of the Poles. Like the people of Seldwyla in Keller's *Novelle*, they were the comfortable burghers who always stayed at home but relished news and visitors from distant places. Stuttgart newspapers printed inspiring editorials, many families offered the refugees room and board, and some young girls cut off their hair as a symbol of mourning for the Poles' fate (cf. III, 135). In 1831 a "Polish Committee" was formed; it was comparable to the "Greek Committee," established in London in 1823, with which Byron was associated and which awakened his interest in the Greek war of liberation. Out of dedication to a similar cause, Lenau was doubtlessly tracing Byron's footsteps in the spiritual sense, although his actual dedication did not match Byron's in scope.

Lenau wrote a group of three "Polenlieder" (I, 79-86) before and shortly after his voyage to America; he wrote a fourth, "Zwei Polen" (I, 245), a dialogue between two refugees, a few years later. The theme recurs in "Klara Hebert" (cf. Chapter 5), and once more in "Die nächtliche Fahrt" (I, 260). What fascinated Lenau was not so much the political issue, not the actuality of the revolution, but the psychological effect of the Poles' expulsion, their solitude and despair in foreign lands.

In "Der Polenflüchtling," one of the three "Polenlieder," an exiled Pole wanders through the African desert, hoping that his heart will soon break. He is unaware of the physical hardships of his situation, the hot sun and the thirst plaguing him, because he is tormented by a greater agony: the loss of Poland. After he sinks to the ground, exhausted, and falls asleep, a squad of mounted Bedouins—nomads themselves—chance upon him. They contemplate the sleeper, see "the sacred marks of battle scars" (*der Narben Heiligtum*) upon his brow and face, and are awed by what they recognize as "the silent majesty of misfortune" (*des Unglücks stille Majestät*). The Bedouins wait for the Pole to awaken and then greet him by singing ancestral songs. The Pole, still half dreaming, imagines that he hears his compatriots on the battlefield of Ostrolenka and is about to draw his sword when he realizes where he is. He drops to the ground, weeping. This final scene depicts another situation recurrent in Lenau's work: the experience of utter frustration.

"Zwei Polen" perpetuates the frustrated attitude. Boleslav, one of the two protagonists, has roamed the seas for seven years, unwilling to set foot on land after the disgrace of Poland. His friend Hippolyt chides him for his attitude of "resting on the thorny pillows of sorrowful inactivity." He asks Boleslav what he would do if he were to discover, through a messenger bird from the homeland, that arms had been taken up again and that his friends were waiting for him. Boleslav replies that no bird is going to come, but that if it did come, he would jump into the sea, and his unfettered spirit would rush to the battlefield as a guiding star for his friends. Boleslav experiences his sorrows more deeply than any other feeling. When Hippolyt excitedly points at a storm cloud in the hope for favorable winds, Boleslav replies, in the final lines of the poem:

Die Winde gehn und kommen,
Die Woge ebbt und flutet,
Doch ewig ohne Hülfe
Die tiefe Wunde blutet!
(I, 249)

("The winds come and go, the wave rises and falls, but eternally and beyond help my deep wound bleeds.")

"Die nächtliche Fahrt" (I, 260) introduces the motif of the Russo-Polish struggle symbolically in a setting of snow and ice and an atmosphere of physical as well as spiritual gelidity. The poem opens with the description of an Eastern European steppe in wintertime. Lenau portrays it as one great tomb, forsaken even by the winds of the heath. A Polish voivode and his coachman travel in a sleigh through the night, pursued by packs of wolves. While the coachman drives the horses frantically, the voivode sits motionless. The horses outrace the wolves, and finally the sleigh stops at an inn. Only now does the reader learn that the voivode is dead, killed by a Russian in a duel. The motif of inactivity and mental paralysis on the part of the Polish exile is here given its final form: death, which at first does not appear for what it really is, but resembles noble bearing coupled with indifference in the face of a nightmarish danger.

The death motif is inherent in both the theme and the imagery of the poem. Early in the poem, Lenau associates ice and snow with the idea of death:

> Nur Schnee und Schnee ringsaus in alle Weiten,
> Nur stiller, keuscher, kalter Tod zu finden.
>
> (I, 260)

("Snow and nothing but snow roundabout in the distance; nothing but silent, chaste, cold death can be found.")

Death is used metaphorically for snow when Lenau says that the forest is "deeply covered by death." Only when the reader is told that the voivode is dead does the snow-death imagery become identified with the theme of the poem. At this point, Lenau carries the symbolism even further. The coachman describes how his master's blood seeped into the snow, forming what Lenau characterizes, in a neologism, as "Bluteis" (blood-ice). It would not melt until spring. After this striking image of a complete solidification of life's blood, Lenau corroborates the symbol in a final parallel between the murderous lead, the voivode's heart, and the snow roundabout. He states that they are of the same icy substance. The poem, in its perfectly balanced oppressiveness, is a representative example of Lenau's art and was considered, according to Schurz, by the poet as one of his finest accomplishments.[12]

IV *Political Engagement*

Lenau sent the manuscript of one of his "Polenlieder"—"In der Schenke"—to Karl Mayer, under the original title "An die Heidelberger Burschen. 29. November" (the anniversary of the Polish revolution). Mayer sent it on to Kerner at whose house it was secretly copied by a visiting clergyman. It was then sent to the editor of *Der Hochwächter*, one of the radical liberal journals that took a special interest in the Polish cause and related political issues. The poem promptly appeared in this journal, but without the knowledge of Lenau or any of his Swabian friends. This, in itself, would not have been cause for alarm, but at the same time (January, 1832) the poem, together with another entitled "Am Grabe des Ministers***" appeared in a Heidelberg periodical, *Microcosmus*. The poems were signed "N. Lenau," the poet's accustomed pseudonym. Apparently the Austrian government did not know Lenau's true identity at that time and had no reason to assume that the poet, who published in Germany exclusively, was an Austro-Hungarian subject. In the unauthorized printing in *Der Hochwächter*, however, the byline read "Von dem edeln Ungarn Lenau" ("by the noble Hungarian, Lenau"). *Der Hochwächter* was considered by the Austrian authorities a highly unsavory and demagogic publication. Lenau's mysterious identification of himself as a Hungarian nobleman might have provided a fruitful lead for the Austrian police in finding out who Lenau was.

Lenau seemed concerned about the unfortunate coincidence. In a letter to Sophie Schwab he outlined the consequences that might possibly result from it: a drawn-out investigation and lawsuit, incarceration, a heavy fine, cancellation of his passport, and strict surveillance by the police. Moreover, he wrote, he felt as silly as a guest at a masquerade, whose face is hidden behind a mask, but on whose back a practical joker has attached a sign with his name (III, 115f.). Lenau was dramatizing the situation, to be sure, but he did have reason to be concerned. Taking sides with Poland against Russia was not the reason for his concern so much as that he had circumvented the law stating that no Austrian subject might publish anything abroad or at home without first submitting the manuscript to the bureau of censorship. Lenau's friends feared the worst. It may be characteristic of Austrian ways and manners of the time that nothing at all happened; the issue of *Der Hochwächter* went unnoticed.

The above incident relates to a particular category of Lenau's themes: his political poems. Lenau's creative career fell into the midst of the *Vormärz* period in Austria, the years between the Congress of Vienna (1815) and the revolution in March, 1848. In Austria, this period was one of political restoration, reactionary in its outlook and anxious to suppress all manifestations of a public will or opinion. The people demanded a constitution, self-government, and free expression of ideas. The mentally incapacitated Emperor Ferdinand I (1793-1875) forbade that the word "constitution" be uttered in his presence, and this rule even applied to his physician's talking about his state of health. The Germans, living in a more liberal atmosphere, looked upon Austria as a police state. One must keep in mind, however, that the methods of suppression had not been developed to the degree they have reached in a modern totalitarian state. There was an extremely cumbersome official hierarchy, a staggering amount of paperwork, and a preponderance of plain stupidity over actual viciousness among the controlling organs.

Grillparzer, the great dramatist of the "Vormärz," tells in his autobiography of a chat he had with an acquaintance of his, a jovial old gentleman and high official in the bureau of censorship. The gentleman cheerfully declared that it was he who had stopped one of Grillparzer's plays, *König Ottokars Glück und Ende,* from being performed and printed. "But was there anything politically controversial in the play?" Grillparzer inquired. The answer: "Nothing at all! But I said to myself: You never know for sure."[13] The poet Count Anton Alexander Auersperg, who wrote scintillating diatribes against the government under the pen-name of Anastasius Grün, was forever plagued by investigations and lawsuits, but he happily continued publishing with a German firm, although his true identity was well known.

Lenau, too, became involved in an extended investigation by the Imperial Chancellery and the police. It dragged on from 1836 until 1843 and occupied a number of government officials much more than it did Lenau. His identity was discovered, finally, not through the efficiency of police detectives, but through an entry in the "Österreichische National-Encyclopädie" which stated bluntly what the poet seemed eager to guard as a secret: that Lenau and Niembsch were the same person. In 1836 he was charged with having edited a "Frühlingsalmanach," an anthology of poems, for Cotta in Stuttgart, without having first secured permission from the Austrian bureau of censorship. Lenau declared that he was a Hungarian subject and not under Austrian jurisdiction. When told that the Hungarian and Austrian laws were identical in such matters, he replied that he had not been aware of the existence of such a law. This statement seems to have been given serious consideration. When asked if he were able to pay the moderate fine of twenty-five guilders should such a fine be imposed, he replied that he was without means (it was generally known that he was well-to-do) and could most certainly not pay the fine. This exchange occupied a span of several years. The case became more and more bogged down in the clogged channels of interoffice communications. Eventually it was shelved when it turned out that one court of higher appeal had returned the dossier to a lower court without indicating a decision.

Another case of government interference involving Lenau should be mentioned, and not only because it is of such stuff as operettas are made of. In 1839, Lenau and twelve other writers, poets, and musicians, including Franz Grillparzer and Johann Strauss the Elder, were elected honorary members of the "Cologne Carnival Society." This group, as its name implies, could not easily be accused of harboring controversial political ambitions. Its members arranged weekly theater parties, humorous recitals, and dances, and intensified their activities somewhat during the winter carnival. A package containing the thirteen gaily embellished honorary diplomas was sent to Vienna, in care of an art dealer. At this point, the police intervened. Austrian subjects were not allowed to join foreign clubs and associations unless the club in question existed with the permission of its national government. However, in the case of the Cologne Carnival Society, it had occurred to no one in Cologne to apply for permission to found it and to no one in Berlin to grant it. By becoming honorary members of the society, the thirteen Austrian artists had clearly violated the letter of the law, but the authorities in Vienna showed their willingness to look into the matter and perhaps grant an exception to the rule.

A secret investigation concerning the nature of the Cologne Carnival Society was begun. A letter that Ignaz Castelli, a literary figure and one of the thirteen persons honored, had written to a friend in Leipzig was intercepted by the police and officially opened. The house of Dr. Ludwig Frankl, a physician, writer, and subsequent biographer of Lenau, was searched by the police, and they took with them everything written and printed they could find. The Austrian ambassador and plenipotentiary to the Court of the King of Prussia, Count Trauttmansdorff, was mobilized. He sent back the reassuring news, supplied to him by the Royal Prussian Ministry of Foreign Affairs, that the Cologne Carnival Society enjoyed the protection of the Prussian police and had never been cause for political concern.

Even Count Joseph Sedlnitzky, Austria's powerful, unbending

police chief, suggested in a confidential report to the Emperor—a monument of officialese—"that permission be granted to surrender the honorary diplomas to the writers and musicians" (. . . *nehme ich mir daher die Freiheit, gehorsamst anzutragen, Eure Majestät dürften allergnädigst geruhen zu erlauben, daß den angeführten Dichtern und Musikern die ihnen von dem Großen Stadt Kölnischen Karnevalsverein zugesendeten Diplome erfolgt werden* . . .). The Imperial Chancellery supported the recommendation of the police chief. Not satisfied, the Office of the Immediate Imperial Privy Councillor requested an expert opinion from the Ministry of the Interior. In due time, it was forthcoming, signed by seven officials including the Emperor's brother, Archduke Franz Karl. The Ministry took exception to Count Sedlnitzky's and the Chancellery's eyebrow-raising liberal attitude. The letter of the law should be adhered to, they advised, especially since the club in question served no educational purpose. The Emperor's decision, given in January, 1840, and signed by him in person, followed the recommendation of the Ministry of the Interior. His Majesty's subjects were not permitted to accept the honorary diplomas of the Cologne Carnival Society.[14]

Hilarious, yes, but also enervating, considering that such experiences recurred constantly, and not only in matters as unimportant as the honorary membership in a social club. The peculiar form of tyranny exercised in Austria in the *Vormärz* period was a contributing factor to Lenau's pervading sense of frustration. It was not a crude tyranny, cynical in the exercise of power; not a bristling despotism that makes revolutionary firebrands out of its subjects, not a lawless dictatorship unscrupulous in its choice of henchmen. It was a quaint, timid tyranny, a tyranny of conservatism with a touch of paternal benevolence. The national authorities were mortally afraid of the ideas that had brought about the French Revolution and the death of a queen who was an Austrian princess. They were eager, in a petty, philistine way, to save Austria from a similar fate. There were voices of dissent even among the ruling classes. Austria's Chancellor, Prince Klemens Metternich, called himself a "liberal"—and justly so, if the term is measured against his eighteenth-century background. In 1842, a book under the title *Österreich und dessen Zukunft* ("Austria and Her Future") appeared anonymously in Hamburg. It was an intelligent and sober appraisal of the political situation and contained level-headed suggestions for reforms, without advocating a revolution. The book caused great excitement in Austria. Lenau characterized it in glowing terms in a letter of February, 1843 (V, 113f.). Several years later, the identity of the author was revealed: Baron Viktor Andrian-Werburg, an erudite and high-ranking government official.

The Austrian regime was not one to instil the people with wild passions—hatred, revenge, the desire to kill. It was too impassive to arouse such strong feelings. There was no one against whom to direct the hatred. The intellectual climate was stultifying, and the general atmosphere was one of hopelessness, but the kind of hopelessness one can live with. There was despair, but it was quiet and resigned. These circumstances were instrumental in forming Lenau's personality, in forming his imagination and psychological make-up. The atmosphere in which he lived contributed to the conception of the symbolic figures he had created: Ahasuerus, the Pole, and the Indian—downtrodden, frustrated, and unable or unwilling to act.

Nevertheless, at times Lenau did raise his voice in the practical political issues of the day, and questions of a sociological or political nature play a certain role in some of his poems. A very early example (1823 or 1824) of what one could call the category of Lenau's political poems is "An einen Tyrannen" (I, 464), an Alcaic ode. The poem shows that the *Hainbund* poets were Lenau's spiritual fathers in this category of literature as much as they were in his nature poetry. The poem contains nothing which points to the political actuality with which Lenau was faced. It is an imitation of the "in tyrannos" poetry of the *Göttinger Hain,* of the Stolberg brothers, Friedrich Matthisson, Friedrich Klopstock, and Christian Daniel Schubart—all of them Lenau's elders by two or three generations. The imagery is borrowed from his models. Lenau evoked the fully equipped literary chamber of horrors of vintage 1780, including the hangman's axe, the slave, blood, the clanging of chains, and the avalanche of skulls. The revolutionary movement of 1830 found no echo in his works. "Am Grabe eines Ministers" (I, 122), written late in 1831, was aimed at Prince Metternich, according to Lenau (III, 109). Its original title read "Am Grabe des Ministers***." Yet there is nothing in the poem pointing to Metternich. It is another exercise in the "in tyrannos" genre and was not highly esteemed by Lenau. It is unlikely that the debonair prince (who was not only a fine judge of literature but enjoyed the best of health) would have been disturbed if he had seen the poem and been told that it was about himself. The minister is portrayed riding along in an allegorical golden carriage of fortune, driving his horses more ruthlessly at the sight of each beggar standing by the wayside. Eventually death, in the guise of a highwayman, steps forward from the woods and ends the journey. There is no mourning:

Das Vaterland mit Lachen and Singen
Hält Wacht an deinem Grab,
(I, 123)

("The fatherland, with laughter and singing, keeps watch at your graveside.")

The period shortly before his voyage to America is usually referred to as Lenau's politically most radical. It is true that he was critical of the Austrian monarchy—almost everyone was—and could be counted among the intellectual liberals, although he was anything but their spokesman. In his literary-political pursuits, he came nowhere near Anastasius Grün, for example, whose poems reflect the atmosphere of the period and, at the same time, observe an ironic distance from the happenings. In his famous "Salonszene" (1831), Grün offered an excellent comment on the Austrians' attitude to freedom. A petitioner stands at Metternich's door, politely waiting to be enchanted by the Prince's gesture of grace. In the end, Grün tells the reader who the petitioner is and what he wants:

Österreichs Volk ist's, offen, wohlerzogen auch und fein,
Sieh, es fleht ganz artig: Dürft' ich wohl so frei sein,
frei zu sein?

("It's Austria's people, openhearted, well-bred, and genteel. Behold, they implore very politely: May I take the liberty of being free?")

Such loving irony was not Lenau's forte. He did not have the patience to examine the subtleties of the reality facing him and to express it as an artist. Only in one poem of that time did Lenau approach the political facts: "Abschied. Lied eines Auswandernden" (I, 121). The subtitle originally read "Lied eines auswandernden Portugiesen" ("Song of an Emigrating Portuguese"). This was a protective measure against Austrian authorities, for it is evident that the Portuguese is Lenau leaving for America. He bids goodbye to his country in strong words:

Sei mir zum letztenmal gegrüßt,
Mein Vaterland, das, feige dumm,
Die Ferse dem Despoten küßt
Und seinem Wink gehorchet stumm.
(I, 121)

("One last goodbye to you, my fatherland, which cowardly and stupidly kisses the heel of the despot and silently obeys his every nod.")

He bids his ship make haste to reach the shores where the divine flame blazes, and implores the sea to take him across the abyss that separates him from freedom. The poems ends:

Du neue Welt, du freie Welt,
An deren blütenreichem Strand
Die Flut der Tyrannei zerschellt,
Ich grüße dich, mein Vaterland!
(I, 122)

("Thou new world, thou free world, on whose flowery shores the tide of tyranny is shattered, I greet thee, my fatherland!")

Thematically, the poem is vaguely applicable to Lenau's own situation. Stylistically, it is of the eighteenth century, even in such details as the poet's use of the archaic form "fleug" instead of "flieg" (fly).

Parallel to Lenau's disillusionment with America went his disenchantment with the idea of political revolt. While living in Economy, Pa., he was exposed to the strong anti-Jacksonian attitude of the members of the Harmony Society. In accordance with a widespread view, they saw in Andrew Jackson's brand of democracy the threatening rise of the rabble and the end of orderly government. Under the influence of the Harmonists, Lenau reversed his political views. Within weeks, he became convinced that the struggle for freedom was sheer folly. In a long lost poem, "An die Ultraliberalen in Deutschland,"[16] he drew a portentous picture of freedom raging uncontrolled, as a warning to his friends in Germany.

The monarchy, he said in the poem, is the symbol of paternal love created by God for the benefit of the "wanderer on lonely, wild paths" (*Wanderer auf den einsam wilden Pfaden*) and the "homeless, gloomy nomad" (*heimatlosen, düsteren Nomaden*). Smash the thrones, he warned, and fall prey to the wintry frost of a republic. In a dream sequence he depicts freedom, an allegorical figure that his compatriots worship because they do not know her true nature:

Ein freches Weib, mit wirren Flatterhaaren,
Kam sie durch jauchzend tolle Pöbelmassen
Auf trümmervollen blutgetränkten Straßen
In rasendem Triumph einhergefahren.

In ihrem Schoße lag mit wildem Schreien
Die junge Brut der schlimmsten Leidenschaften,
Die gierig ihrer Mutter Brüste rafften
Und sogen mit entsetzlichem Gedeihen.

("An insolent woman, her disheveled hair flying wildly, she rode in raving triumph through cheering, frantic masses of rabble, through streets filled with ruins and drenched with blood. In her lap, with wild screams, lay the young brood of the worst passions, greedily grasping at their mother's breasts, drinking and thriving dreadfully.")

She incites the masses to pluck the crosses from the church steeples, to sweep everything that was sacred into one great pile and drown it all in rivers of blood. Shall this harpy dwell upon Germany's soil? the poet asks his countrymen.

The reversal of Lenau's attitude could not have been more complete, so that one must conclude that Lenau's original political radicalism could not have been very deepseated. The imagery used in his portrayal of freedom's excesses is as hackneyed as that employed in his radical liberal poems. In fact, they resemble each other. The bloodthirsty images as such were more important to Lenau than the ideas he conveyed through them. He revels in the horrible as such. The discussion of some of Lenau's long epic poems in subsequent chapters will corroborate this conclusion.

On his return from America, Lenau adhered for many years to his newly gained mistrust of political freedom, even though he never again expressed himself as strongly as in the quoted poem. In company he averred that his stay in America had cured him "of the chimera of freedom and independence." He had convinced himself, he said, that "true freedom can only live within our own hearts."[17] The poem "Protest" (I, 484), written shortly after his return, reiterates some of the ideas of "An die Ultraliberalen in Deutschland," without, however, introducing the allegorical figure of freedom. He wrote:

When I profess to hate conspiracies and rascals hiding in the garb of the people's champions; when I consider monarchies a heavenly gift and a shelter to forsaken nations, do not believe that I love without a question our own present kings."

Although both poems remained unpublished, the second is clearly an attempt to take back some of the excessiveness exhibited in the first.

The thin trickle of Lenau's political poetry almost ends here. Political issues do come up in his long epic poems, even though marginally. In *Faust,* Lenau draws a caricature of an absolutistic court, and in *Savonarola* the protagonist beseeches Lorenzo de' Medici to give freedom to the people of Florence. Only toward the end of his career, in *Die Albigenser*, does the issue of freedom from political oppression receive a more dominant position. Among the shorter poems of the later years, there are only a few that touch on political themes. Lenau's interest in the outside world was not great enough to make him an ardent political champion.

CHAPTER 5

Five Lyric-Epic Cycles

LENAU wrote five works of medium length—longer than his lyrical poems and shorter than his epic-dramatic works. They are composed in the form of lyrical cycles, but their subject matter is epic in nature. Each is subdivided into units of approximately the length of a ballad.

The earliest of these cycles is "Klara Hebert. Ein Romanzenkranz" (I, 175-203), written in 1831. A highly romantic piece, it combines Lenau's previously discussed motif of the Pole with that of the prisoner.

During a visit, a Polish prince, Johann Kasimir, falls in love with Klara, the daughter of an innkeeper in the Provence. Subsequently, he is thrown into a dungeon because he had not paid royal homage to Cardinal Richelieu, minister of France. In the guise of a page boy, and without Kasimir's knowledge, Klara manages to remain near the prince. When two emissaries of Richelieu try to kill the prince, she thwarts the attempt, saves Kasimir's life, and is seriously wounded. While she recovers, Kasimir is released from prison by the intervention of his brother, the King of Poland. On leaving, he espies Klara in the crowd, raises her to her feet—she had fainted—and entrusts her to the protection of a French nobleman. Later he returns and takes Klara as his wife.

Lenau's source was a novel, *Der gallische Kerker* (1827), by a now forgotten author, Alexander von Oppeln-Bronikowski, a minor imitator of Sir Walter Scott and widely read in his day. There is a strong resemblance between the libretto of Beethoven's *Fidelio* and this novel. It is based, very vaguely, on actual historical events.[1] In Lenau's source, the heroine was a gay, cunning southern French girl. He turned her into a wide-eyed, sentimental maiden, somewhat reminiscent of Klärchen in Goethe's *Egmont*. Klara's foremost characteristic is her absolute devotion to Kasimir, her unquestioned willingness to sacrifice herself for him without attracting his attention. In fact, sacrificial subordination is the dominant idea of the entire cycle and is corroborated by the imagery. Early in the poem, Lenau describes the town of Cisteron, the place of action:

Furchtsam ruht am Fuß des Berges
Städtchen Cisteron geschmieget,
Wie zu des Gebieters Füßen
Weinend eine Sklavin lieget.
(I, 176)

("Timidly nestling at the foot of the mountain, rests the town of Cisteron, as a slave girl would lie weeping at her master's feet.")

This image will be readily associated with Klara's attitude toward Kasimir. Toward the end of the cycle, it is transferred into the physical realm and becomes part of the actual events: Klara faints and lies prostrate before Kasimir on a marble staircase. In describing the location of the prison—it is high on a cliff—Lenau reminds the reader that the dungeon was at one time a pagan temple. Thus the scene is set for the action. An atmosphere is created, and associations are evoked. By confirming the main idea through imagery, the poet achieves a great unity in this work, notwithstanding the modest aim that he had, on the whole, set for himself. An obvious comparison is that between "Klara Hebert" and Heinrich von Kleist's play *Käthchen von Heilbronn*. Both themes deal with a loving maiden's unquestioning subordination, but neither work, while successful within its limited scope, does full honor to its poet.

The term *Romanze* in the subtitle of the cycle denotes a special form of the ballad in German. It deals with love, and is, in its simple form, reminiscent of folk songs and the world of fairy tales. Goethe called his famous "Es war ein König in Thule" a *Romanze*. The strophic form used in Lenau's cycle is that of the folk song: four lines of tetrameters with an a b c b rhyme scheme. Lenau was most successful in portraying Klara's love and devotion, her yearning for the prince, and the wedding which takes place in the former dungeon. He introduced no subtleties that would not be appropriate to the form of the *Romanze*. Less successful are those passages in which the poet was forced to deal with the world of intrigues and politics, a world he did not know at all. There he resorted to clichés. The portrayal of Kasimir combines, in a fashion characteristic of Lenau, heroic and melancholic aspects. His features bespeak "great seriousness and sweet melancholy" (*tiefen Ernst und süße Schwermut*), but his flashing eyes betray high spirits and courage. When his jailers approach him rudely, mistaking his quiet composure for timidity, and demand his sword in the name of the king, he flares up and thunders at them that the king should come and get it. When a group of soldiers approach to disarm him by force, he draws his sword and puts them to rout.

Lenau was strongly inclined to introduce into his works the stance of rapacious heroism wherever it was possible. In his source the intervention of the Polish King with Louis XIII of France on behalf of Kasimir is described as an example of diplomatic skill and finesse. But Lenau has the messengers enter the castle of St. Germain with bloodied spurs, and they fling insults and threats at the King of France; whereupon the King, frightened and embarrassed, not very credibly gives the order to set the prince free. The scene shows that Lenau, despite his deep insight into the psyche of one individual, showed little subtlety in the portrayal of the psychological interaction of several individuals. This applies to his life as well. It is not surprising, for example, that Lenau and Grillparzer, the great portrayer of human interaction, while frequenting the same café in Vienna and seeing each other constantly, were never able to find a common denominator to their interests and never talked to each other at length. Their personal make-up, as well as their artistic propensity, were diametrically opposed.

"Die Marionetten. Nachtstück" (I, 204-217) was begun late in 1831 and finished aboard ship during the voyage to America, in the fall of 1833. Written in terza rimas, the cycle consists of three parts ("Gesänge"). If the idea in "Klara Hebert" could be summarized as a woman's devotion, in "Die Marionetten" it is grief and insane vengefulness—ideas of central importance in Lenau's imagination. He portrayed them in a wide range of intensity in this work.

Amidst a fearful scenery, the narrator encounters a hermit who relates to him his life's story. He loved Maria, the daughter of Count Roberto, his overlord, whom he had accompanied in many campaigns. The count, who had finally settled down in a lonely castle near the hermit's present abode, would have granted him Maria's hand. Maria, however, was reluctant, postponed her decision, and finally fell prey to a young visitor, Lorenzo, who seduced and then forsook her. She died of sorrow, and her father's grief over her death is so great that he loses control over his mind.

Unable to trace Lorenzo and take revenge on him, Count Roberto devises an eery puppet play with characters from real life. Each performance ends with the killing of the Lorenzo puppet. Years later, Lorenzo's son Antonio visits the castle by chance. He resembles his father closely and is immediately put in chains by Roberto who, in his demented state, is certain that he is dealing with Lorenzo. Word of his son's fate and whereabouts reaches Lorenzo, and he rushes to Roberto's castle to save his son. He arrives in time to see a performance of Roberto's puppet play and the decapitation of the puppet representing him. Roberto welcomes the guest and offers to repeat the show for Lorenzo's pleasure. The marionettes begin to dance. But now a new figure enters the stage, with an awkward gait and suspended on chains: Antonio's corpse. Roberto comments on the scene in a mock-tragic sermon, and Lorenzo dies of sudden shock. Having ended his story, the hermit leaves. The narrator is uncertain whether what he heard was reality or dream.

Lenau's source for this cycle is a mystery. He never mentioned it in letters or in conversation. A number of details in the plot, including the name Lorenzo, are reminiscent of Thomas Kyd's *Spanish Tragedy* (c. 1586), but there is no further indication that Lenau knew it.[2] As in "Klara Hebert," the poet set the right atmosphere for the poem in the opening description of the landscape. "Mute, immeasurable, wild mourning" (*stummes, unermeßlich wildes Trauern*) is the impression which the dismal, haunting nature scene conveys to the narrator and which is then transferred to the subject-matter of the poem. More specifically, the cycle begins and ends with the image of a tuft of lamb's wool hanging on a bush, with a satiated vulture circling overhead. Lenau's intended association of this image with the action of the poem is obvious.

Although the import of the poem is contrary to that of "Klara Hebert," there is a similarity in the figures of the young women and the effects of the appearance of their respective partners on them: They are entirely at their mercy. In the present cycle—more in line with Lenau's general patterns of imagination—the events take a tragic turn. The work is subtitled "Nachtstück" ("Nocturne"), evidently under the influence of E.T.A. Hoffmann's grotesque *Nachtstücke* (1817). The hero, Antonio, has unmistakably Byronic characteristics. He is proud, quick, and bold, wears a hunter's outfit, carries a rifle, and is first seen climbing a mountain on his way to Roberto's castle. His expression is foreboding in the Byronic manner:

> Die Stirne brütend und gewitterschwül,
> Die Augen zwei gefangne Blitze brennen;
> Doch lag es um die Lippen ihm so kühl,
> Ein Rätsel, unerfreulich zu erkennen.
> Die Blässe sprach: dies Herz hat keinen Frieden;
> (I, 209)

("His brow brooding and with the oppressive air of an approaching storm, his eyes burning like two captured flashes of lightning; yet there was a coolness around his lips, an enigma unpleasant to decipher. His pallor revealed: there is no peace in this heart.")

Antonio resembles Lenau's Faust, and both are examples of the Byronic "homme fatal." The portrayal of grief in all its facets was Lenau's main concern when he composed the cycle. Telling the story, he "rips away the dressing of time to expose his heart's wound" (I, 206)—a recurrent image in Lenau's works—and adjures the "god of pain" to give him his support. His feelings for Maria are expressed in terms of wounds. Her glances inflict wounds upon him that will heal only when he draws his last breath. Although he did not win her love, he had no desire ever to recover from these wounds. Roberto's grief manifests itself in a different way. Like several of Lenau's characters, he is turned into a psychopath by an overpowering mental anguish.

The cycle "Mischka" (I, 388-403) consists of two poems, "Mischka an der Theiss" and "Mischka an der Marosch."[3] The setting of the cycle is Hungary, and its theme is the fate of a gypsy fiddler and his daughter. The first poem, written in 1834, is a glorification of gypsy life and gypsy music, comparable to "Die Werbung." It evokes better than any other of Lenau's poems the vivacious yet melancholy world of Hussars and gypsies, horseback rides through the steppes, and the abandon induced by the magic of dance music. The poem is a masterpiece of sound effects and recreates successfully the sweet and fiery passion of gypsy music. The content matter is simple: Hussars enter a tavern, and Mischka and his band play for them. With great power and beauty they play tunes of bygone glory and evoke before the Hussars' inner eyes scenes of battles against the Turks, their traditional enemies. Entranced, they rush into the night, ready to attack, but find nothing but a peaceful moon and the rustling waters of the Tisza River. Many of the lines in the poem are effective by their sound alone. Deprived of it, as in a translation, they would lose their interest because they say little:

> Manche Geige mag im schönen
> Lande der Magyaren tönen,
> Doch im Land die Geige keiner
> Spielt wie Mischka, der Zigeuner.
> (I, 390)

("Many a violin may sound in the beautiful land of the Hungarians; but in the whole country no one plays the violin as does Mischka the gypsy.")

What saves such lines, in the original, from turning into doggerels of the kind Wilhelm Busch liked to concoct is their urgent, stacatto beat, their musicality and silky luxuriance—qualities that are atmospheric and are far removed from the conceptual.

The second part of the cycle, "Mischka an der Marosch," written in 1842, eight years after the first, is subdivided into four sections and tells a story. Mischka has moved on to the Marosch River and built himself a flimsy cottage, not meant to last longer than the time he can tolerate staying in one place. The cottage gives shelter to him and his daughter, Mira, who has been under his care since the death of Mischka's beloved wife. From here on, the cycle is thematically related to "Die Marionetten." The seducer, a young count from nearby appears. Winning Mira through irresistible flattery, he leaves her after a few days. Mira wanders aimlessly through the forests and dies amidst the rushes, by the side of a pond (a favorite Lenau setting).

Mischka's revenge has aspects of the supernatural often attributed to gypsies in folklore. He cuts hair from the tail of the count's fastest horse with which to string his bow, and he curses the horse's hooves. Invited to play at the count's wedding feast, Mischka asks for the privilege of presenting a violin solo, especially composed by him for the occasion. What he plays is his child's grief and death, and his revenge. The seducer and the guests can hear the kindling fire of first love, the ecstasies of the bridal night, the lamentations of the forsaken girl, her vain search for her lover, her call for help to the gods, and her escape into death. When the playing stops, the young bride steals away, weeping, she knows not why. The count, driven by an unknown force, gallops away on his horse, falls and is killed. On the morning after, a shepherd boy watches the gypsy musician bury his violin in Mira's grave. It is the last time Mischka is seen.

Possibly Lenau was inspired to write the second poem of the cycle, "Mischka an der Marosch," by an undistinguished long epic poem by Karl Beck (1817-1879), *Jankó, der ungarische Roßhirt* (1841). Beck, now forgotten, was another German-speaking poet from Hungary and an acquaintance of Lenau's. In his poem, which, in turn, shows the influence of Kleist's novelle *Michael Kohlhaas,* the hero kills a count who had seduced his wife, then burns his castle. He becomes an outlaw and bandit, and dies on the gallows.

Although the two parts of Lenau's cycle were written at different times, they are closely connected. The first poem creates the necessary atmosphere and introduces the theme of music's magic power. Hussars, hearing Mischka's martial music, imagine that they are in battle. In the first poem, Lenau handled the theme playfully. In the second, he raised it into the realm of the demonic. "Mischka an der Marosch" is remarkable for its balladlike qualities and its sustained narrative power. Ordinarily the lyricist Lenau did not excel in these matters. By virtue of both its theme and form, the Mischka cycle is part of the Romantic tradition. It is one of Lenau's most successful treatments of the gypsy motif.

The cycle "Anna" (I, 372-386), written in 1838 and consisting of five poems, has the sub-title "Nach einer schwedischen Sage" ("After a Swedish Legend"). It is the legend of the woman who, for the sake of retaining her beauty, wants to remain childless, makes an agreement with an evil spirit and has her wish in exchange for her shadow. The theme, probably Scandinavian in origin, is extant in many versions[4] and was used as recently as 1919 in Hugo von Hofmannsthal's *Die Frau ohne Schatten.* Lenau had heard the legend from an acquaintance, the Swedish philologist and aesthetician Karl August Hagberg (1810-1864). Lenau's version shows few elements that could be called characteristically his own, but the theme held a morbid fascination for him on personal grounds. In his endless, thwarted love for Sophie Löwenthal, he often felt that he was deprived of a home and a family, and he resented the fact that her children were not his children.

In a letter, Lenau referred to this poem as a cycle of

Romanzen (IV, 303). The form and, to a large extent, the content justify the term. Fairy tale motifs abound in the work. It begins with an image of narcissism:

Anna steht in sich versunken,
Blicket in den See hinein,
Weidet, eigner Schönheit trunken,
Sich an ihrem Widerschein.
(I, 372)

("Absorbed in herself, Anna stands and gazes into the lake. Intoxicated with her own beauty, she revels in her own reflection.")

The more delight she takes in her image, the more beautiful she becomes; and her greater beauty adds to her enchantment. But soon a wind comes up, clouds the surface, ripples the water, and makes Anna's image fade. This opening scene anticipates the action of the cycle, a recurrent device in Lenau's longer poems. As Anna mourns her vanished image, an old woman appears and offers her services. She can help Anna remain beautiful forever by making her infertile. Anna agrees to return to her by the time she is ready to take a husband. The appearance of her suitor is described strictly in the fairy-tale tradition. A knight stands before her window, playing the zither and singing to her:

Hab ein Schloß und finstre Wälder,
Berge hab ich, reich an Erz,
Muntre Herden, goldne Felder,
Und nach dir ein krankes Herz!
(I, 375)

("I have a castle and dark forests; I have mountains rich with ore; I have lively herds of cattle, golden fields, and a heart aching for you.")

He leaves a ring on a rose branch and rides away. Anna takes the ring and meets with the old woman who had been waiting in the bushes. They cross a heath and enter a windmill. The old woman picks seven grains of wheat from a bag—the number of children Anna would have had—and drops them, one by one, through Anna's ring onto the grindstone of the mill. Whenever a grain falls, a gust of wind sets the mill into motion, and the short wail of an infant is heard from below. Only seven years later does the husband discover the missing shadow during a horseback ride in bright moonlight. Anna confesses. He casts her out, exclaiming that she will not be forgiven just as surely as no roses will grow from the floor of the entrance hall to his castle. For the next seven years, Anna roams through the wilderness. In the end, she dies and is forgiven by the souls of her unborn children.

The cycle "Johannes Ziska" (I, 426-445), consisting of nine poems, was begun in 1838 or 1839 and completed in 1842 or 1843. Its genesis is unusual. After finishing his *Faust* in 1836, Lenau planned an extensive epic trilogy about Jan Hus, Girolamo Savonarola, and Ulrich von Hutten. He started with the second, and concluded his *Savonarola* a year later. In June, 1837, he began to read historical works in preparation for a poem on Jan Hus, the Bohemian religious reformer and follower of John Wycliffe, who was burned in Constance after refusing to recant his doctrine that St. Peter was not the head of the Christian Church. After his death, a religious war broke out in Bohemia between his followers and Sigismund, the Holy Roman Emperor. Lenau soon lost his enthusiasm for the planned work. The subject matter had become distasteful to him, the Hussites began to appear like common murderers (IV, 125), and he found the never-ending battle din monotonous (IV, 270). Only one character continued to fascinate him, and surprisingly so, since the battle din was loudest where he was: Jan Žižka[5] (?-1424), the brilliant, ruthless military leader of the Taborites, the more extreme faction of the Hussites. Lenau decided on a shorter cycle of *Romanzen* ("Romanzenkranz," [IV, 270]) on Ziska instead of a long poem on the Hussite Wars in general. In one of his sources, Jacques Lenfant's *Histoire de la guerre des Hussites et du conceil de Basle* (Amsterdam, 1731), he had found a picture of the Hussite leader. He commented on it in a letter to Max Löwenthal, saying that he was revelling in Ziska's fearsome features, and that each of them had inspired him to write a canto of his poem (IV, 257-258). A note to Sophie Löwenthal throws light on the reason for Lenau's enthusiasm for Ziska. He considered the character a vehicle for the release of his own pent-up aggression:

> It makes me feel good to have found material like Ziska, the hero of the Hussite Wars. With him, I can be ruthless, and can give free rein to my ill temper. Long restrained furies will break loose, and I will convey such disdain of humanity that many a reader will wish to have his own soul physically before him so that he can spit at it. (IV, 113).

"Ziska" was written during the same year as *Die Albigenser* (cf. Chapter 7), the epic poem about a religious war in southern France. In many respects, it is an outgrowth and extension of the longer work. Theme and imagery are related, and so is the poet's attitude. He was reacting against his own period of religious mysticism, visible in *Savonarola,* by indulging in an unrestrained exhibition of violence in his subsequent works.

Lenau tried to draw a superhuman figure in his protagonist. Ziska spurns all human emotions. When his former beloved, now frail and wilting, sends word begging him to return to her, he replies that she should die as a sacrificial offering in the name of freedom. To his enemies he appears as the incarnation of death. He was born in the depth of a forest during a raging storm. He says that the storm was his mother's midwife and poured a flame of lightning over his head as a blessing. Hail struck her laboring womb to strengthen him against the enemies' missiles. Thunder was his "first hearing," and storm his first breath. In the crashing of thunder, Ziska hears a spirit related to his own soul.

There is no historical progression in the sequence of the nine cantos or parts. Some relate Ziska's thoughts; some are scenes from the Hussites' camp; one is a contemplation on the effect of blindness; one meditates on death; and one depicts the dying hero. In the poem on man's reaction to blindness (Ziska lost both eyes), Lenau showed subtlety and originality. Pain will enter the heart of a blind man twice as cruelly, he wrote, because he is excluded from the consolation of a quiet smile that could ease his burden.

> Tiefer stürzt der Schmerz beim Anruf
> Gleich dem Hirsche, dem erschrocknen,
> In die Wildnis; doch das stumme
> Lächeln kann das Auge trocknen.
> (I, 436)

("Like a frightened stag, pain will rush into desolate wilderness at a call; but a silent smile can dry the eye.")

The question of man's reaction to pain is one that Lenau understood, one he could speak of with poetic truth. Whenever he tries to show strength and defiance, on the other hand, his lines are forced and ring untrue. And yet, the cycle is memorable for the very reason that it is an artistic failure. Ziska's paroxysms of violence are fruitless, and his display of force does not hide the underlying sense of frustration. The blind general, trying to conduct the battle from a cart with the help of two officers who describe to him every turn of events, is a symbol of this sense of futility. Several of the cantos show Ziska in a state of suspension, waiting to act or unable to act. Not unlike Holofernes in Hebbel's *Judith* (1839), he speaks more about his strength than he shows himself strong. At times, Ziska even gives himself to dreaming about doing things he cannot do. After the poet has associated him with the image of lightning, Ziska regrets the transiency of its flash and adds:

> Könnt ich doch hier an die Tanne
> Nageln ihn mit meinem Schwert!
> (I, 432)

("I wish I could nail it to this pinetree with my sword!")

He dreams of extending his power: "I wish I could fly like clouds at night in an unhampered course! I wish I could shoot my deadly bolts at the sinners in their redoubts!" In the end, Ziska dies not on the battlefield, but of the plague. He wills that his skin be used as a drum skin, a desire which is, in effect, another attempt at self-perpetuation. He dies dreaming of battles, of smashing the heads of Imperial soldiers, of thrusting his frost-covered lance deep into their entrails.

In the final analysis, Lenau's hero is not the paragon of strength whom the poet set out to draw. At every step he betrays the frailty of his creator, the poet, who could conceive of victorious power only in the form of wishful dreams and magniloquence.

CHAPTER 6

The Sinful Sufferer and the Holy Vandal: Faust *and* Savonarola

I Faust

IN November, 1833, shortly after his return from America, Lenau wrote to Georg Reinbeck in Stuttgart that he was working on a "rhapsody" entitled *Faust*. "The fact that Goethe wrote a *Faust*," he told Reinbeck, "does not deter me. Faust is a common property of mankind, not a monopoly of Goethe" (III, 242). It is true that writing a *Faust* after Goethe need not be considered an "*Ilias* post Homerum." The theme of man's relationship with the universe, the balance of powers between him and the world is so general and all-embracing that no two poets will treat it alike. Goethe's version was merely one among many that originated in the Storm and Stress movement and gave expression to the newly felt conflict between the controlling intellect and raw vitality, between culture and nature, restriction and abandon. The first part of Goethe's *Faust* did not appear until 1808. The second was published posthumously in 1832. There were treatments of the theme by Friedrich Maximilian Klinger (1752-1831), Friedrich (Maler) Müller (1749-1825), and by such minor figures as Johann Friedrich Schink, Count Soden, and August Klingemann.[1] Several decades later, Achim von Arnim (1781-1831) suggested that every poet write his own *Faust* and give voice to his individual experience of revolt, doom, or salvation. Of Lenau's contemporaries, Franz Grillparzer, Heinrich Heine, Adelbert von Chamisso, Christian Dietrich Grabbe, and half a dozen lesser poets wrote, or at least began to write, their *Faust*.

In 1817, Byron's *Manfred* appeared, strongly influenced by the first part of Goethe's *Faust* and highly praised by Goethe. Whereas Goethe had followed the older Faust tradition by showing his protagonist in his search for a knowledge hidden from other mortals, Byron's hero does not seek knowledge but oblivion. What the spirits offer him—sovereignty, power over the earth, control of the elements—does not entice him. He wants forgetfulness of what is within him. Impatient with one spirit who offers him "length of days," he shouts back that his days are too long already. Byron's work influenced Lenau's more than any of the other versions of the legend. In terms of individual motifs, Lenau's poem is indebted to a number of Fausts, ranging from the old chapbook of 1587[2] to Goethe's completed play, but the attitude of his protagonist is most closely related to that of Manfred.

Lenau planned a *Faust* as early as 1823, but ten years passed before he began to work on it. The poem appeared in 1836 and was received with great praise as well as severe criticism.

At the time, a fierce conflict raged in the field of theology between Orthodoxy and a new version of eighteenth-century deism exemplified by David Friedrich Strauss, whose main work, *The Life of Jesus,* appeared in 1835.[3] The issue grew even more complicated when the politically reactionary groups joined forces with the champions of religious restoration. Conversely, liberalism assumed a strongly anticlerical attitude. Few writers were willing, or able, to stay aloof from the struggle. Lenau fluctuated between the forces. After a halfhearted effort to find a place in the liberal camp in Vienna, he associated with the Swabian Poets in Stuttgart, a group without political interests but with a strictly orthodox religious outlook. Lenau was antagonistic toward Heinrich Heine and the liberal Young Germans, the group of politically active writers who battled everything that smacked of Romanticism, provincialism, and clericalism, and were on all counts opposed to the Stuttgart circle. During his stay in America, he was in close contact with the members of the Pietistic Harmony Society in Pennsylvania. Lenau's voice could be heard in the chorus of anti-Goethe polemicists, led by the Stuttgart critic and editor of the influential *Literaturblatt,* Wolfgang Menzel. While being close to the Swabian Poets, Lenau chided Goethe for his Hellenistic attitude and accused him of having done a great disservice to German literature.

When Lenau's *Faust* appeared, the atmosphere was charged. The anti-Goethean exponents of religious orthodoxy, although they could never consider Lenau completely as one of their own and forever tried to strengthen the ties between him and themselves, expected his poem to be an answer of sort to Goethe's, and the Young Germans were waiting to pounce on him.

It is difficult to define the form of the work. Lyric passages and epic descriptions alternate with dialogues that are not really dramatic but rather exchanges of ideas between two or more characters. Various literary genres are blended in this work, and the result is a form that is unique in Lenau's time. Only much later, in the age of Symbolism, do comparable creations occur, as for example in William Butler Yeats' *The Wanderings of Oisin* (=Ossian), written in 1889, and in young Hofmannsthal's playlets. Lenau's choice of so hybrid a form is significant and closely connected with the spiritual nature of the work which is a portrayal of the inner experiences of the protagonist, who, in turn, is an extension of the poet. In kaleidoscopic episodes his inner life is unrolled, and the outer form of each scene depends on its atmosphere. There is no unity and little coherence in the external action. The work, not constructed as a drama, is, rather, a "Seelendrama"—a drama of the soul—without being a play. Faust is the pivot of the poem. Other characters merely come and go and do not contribute by developing a plot. Lenau referred to his *Faust*, vaguely, as a "rhapsody" (see chapter opening); Eduard Castle suggested the term "symphonische Dichtung" (VI, 517). Both terms obscure rather than elucidate the issue, but they do justice to one aspect of the work, namely its atmospheric, musical quality. It is not by accident that two of Lenau's longer works have been chosen as the bases for what is often classified as program music. Franz Liszt was inspired by *Faust* to write both his *Faust Symphony* and *Mephisto Waltz*, and Richard Strauss subtitled his *Don Juan* "Tondichtung nach Nikolaus Lenau" ("Tone Poem after Nikolaus Lenau"). Strauss even had quotations from Lenau's *Don Juan* printed in his score. The open, episodic structure of Lenau's longer poems is akin to the nature of program music, and it is easy to see how it could impress composers.

Faust consists of twenty-three parts or scenes, most of them in rhymed iambic tetrameter and pentameter, each with a title, each from one to twelve printed pages in length. Like Goethe, Lenau did not compose them in their final order, but began with the scenes that interested him most, then added others and arranged them. The action is simple: Faust enters into a pact with the devil, selling him his soul in exchange for knowledge, power, and riches. In the end, in contrast to Goethe's work, the devil gets what he has bargained for. Like Goethe's Faust, Lenau's is a scholar and a scientist rebelling against the limitations of his discipline. On a subtler level, however, the issues are more complex than those in Goethe's *Faust*.

The opening, to be sure, is well within the Faust tradition and is, in fact, strongly inspired by Byron's *Manfred*. In this scene, entitled "Morgengang," Faust climbs a perilous mountain in an attempt to escape physically from the doubts that beset him. The sound of church bells from the valley offers no consolation; they merely signify the helpless outcry of those who would like to believe. Their sound makes Faust realize that he is without faith. While he climbs higher, where no sound from below can reach him, a stone from under his foot gives way, and he falls. As he plunges, he is saved by a sinister-looking hunter. (In Byron's poem, the rescuer is a chamois hunter; in Lenau's, he is the devil.) He disappears without saying a word. When he approaches Faust a second time he comes as a visiting scientist, calling on the famous Faust who, once again, is dissecting bodies in his laboratory in the search for the secret of life. The discussion between Faust and Wagner, his assistant, is indebted to Goethe's work.[4] In his dispute with Mephistopheles, Faust speaks of his own dilemma while characterizing the fate of all men: Time, seen as a stern, shrouded slave of unknown forces, hounds man from the womb of his mother to the womb of his grave. Time remains silent to all questions while rushing man on through the darkness of his existence. Within himself, Faust feels a host of forces, mysterious, despotic, ever burning, pursuing aims of which his conscious mind knows nothing and wants no part. He sees himself "excluded from himself" and forever teased and torn. The image he uses in describing his spiritual situation is strikingly modern:

> Ein Fremdling ohne Ziel und Vaterland,
> Indem ich schwindelnd, strauchelnd fort mich quäle
> Zwischen dem dunkeln Abgrund meiner Seele
> Und dieser Welt verschloßner Felsenwand,
> Auf des Bewußtseins schmalem, schwankem Stege,
> (II, 7)

("A stranger without aim and abode, I plod on, staggering and with my senses reeling, between the dark abyss of my soul and the impenetrable cliff of the world, on the narrow, precarious footbridge of consciousness.")

At this point, Faust is no longer a symbol of intellectual revolt, trying to break through the limitations set to human knowledge. What tortures him is not his inability to transcend human bounds, but, more fundamentally, the failure to come to terms with life as it presents itself to him. He feels that he is not fully part of this world; he is a stranger who follows a perilous course, groping his way along the wall of rock that separates him from reality. He is aware and afraid of the forces of the unconscious—a modern trait that makes a most unexpected appearance in a work published in 1836—without, at the same time, being able to find a firm foothold in his own consciousness. In short, existence in itself has become problematic. When modern critics refer to Lenau's works as early harbingers of existentialist ideas, there is justification in this claim insofar as some of Lenau's protagonists embark on a search for themselves and for their inner identity. Faust exemplifies this attitude most clearly. It cannot be found in any of Lenau's models, if one discounts a slight tendency of this kind in Byron's *Manfred.* But Manfred searches for self-oblivion, whereas Faust, in this sense true to earlier versions of the legend, wants knowledge, if only self-knowledge.

When Goethe's Faust enters upon his pact, the terms are clearly established. Faust searches for a moment of happiness. If he should ever experience a moment so beautiful that he will want it to last, the devil may take him. They agree even on the words Faust will use to express his desire for the perpetuation of the moment of contentment. The arrangement which Lenau's Faust makes, however, lacks this precision completely. Mephistopheles calls the Creator man's "enemy," since He placed man into an eternal night, and challenges Faust to obtain truth through guilt. What this "truth" is—the essence of life or of the universe, or merely an insight into the purpose of man's existence—is never stated. On their third encounter, Faust and Mephistopheles conclude their pact. Faust demands that the devil "lead him to truth so that he may look into truth's countenance" (II, 18). Mephistopheles is willing to agree on these terms but invites Faust, in an enigmatic forewarning, to hang himself on the nearest branch; at the same time, he admits the unreasonableness of this request, since his victim cannot possibly see the logic behind it. Thus Mephistopheles sets his terms and Faust accepts them. Faust becomes the devil's helper for the rest of his earthly days while receiving from him "truth" as well as fame and glory, power and riches. After Faust's death, his soul should go to the devil. The contract is signed with Faust's blood.

As the next scenes unfold, the reader is soon forced to draw a conclusion: Faust has signed away his soul without knowing for what. This is, in effect, the most striking aspect of the work. Faust fails as hopelessly to come to terms with his own fate after signing the pact as before. He does not get what he wanted, and, what is worse, he seems to have lost sight of it. Originally he was not interested in power and riches, but Mephistopheles offers these, too, and they are thrown into the bargain. Now they have gained central importance.

Throughout the rest of the poem, no more mention of truth and knowledge is made. Faust is seen exercising his power and committing deeds that show him as the devil's helper, as he had agreed to be. But he is never shown obtaining truth or even pursuing it. In this respect, Lenau's *Faust* is unique among all the versions of the legend in world literature.

It has been said of Goethe's *Faust* that the entire Gretchen episode, despite its beauty and its central position in the first part of the play, has nothing to do with the Faust problem and, if measured against the idea of the work, is a waste. In the case of Lenau's *Faust,* one may say that everything that follows the signing of the pact has little connection with the idea of the poem, and has nothing at all to do with Faust's original quest. Such lack of continuity in the action could be rated as a flaw, but within Lenau's works as a whole it assumes significance and may be taken as another manifestation—perhaps an unconscious one—of Lenau's most intimate spiritual experiences. The patterns of vanishing, fleeing, and slipping away, the motifs of transiency and cessation recur endlessly in his poetry. When his Faust loses sight of an idea that was vague to begin with, and spends the rest of his life up to the very hour of his suicide in aimless pursuit of things that do not really matter to him, Lenau has drawn another image of the inertia and stultification that beset him so strongly and never ceased to fire his poetic imagination.

Faust, usually accompanied by Mephistopheles, lives through a number of adventures that are made possible by the power he commands. In each of these scenes, Faust is shown as haughty, ruthless, and destructive, indifferent to the fate of others, and yet without taking pleasure in his deeds. There can be no doubt that he is the devil's helper, though a joyless one. He and the devil have certain qualities in common and appear to be cut from the same cloth. In their immense pride they both had aspired to resemble God. Faust remembers how, even as an altar boy, he desired to be the God whom he had to serve. Mephistopheles is traditionally the figure of the fallen, rebellious angel. Rejected, Faust and Mephistopheles have taken the position diametrically opposed to the Creator and have become "anticreators," destroying instead of making. Contemplating his plans, the devil says:

> So will Verstoßner ich mein Leiden kühlen,
> Verderbend mich als Gegenschöpfer fühlen.
> (II, 28)

("Thus I, the outcast, will soothe my sorrows by setting myself up as a destructive anticreator.")

Faust follows suit and helps the devil in his destructive ways, while being destroyed by him.

The violent aspect is only one side of Faust's nature. Interspersed between the scenes of murder and seduction are spells of deep despair and quiet resignation. In fact, Faust constantly fluctuates between these two aspects of his personality. In one scene, "Der nächtliche Zug" (II, 58-60), Faust encounters a religious procession late at night and is entranced by the music they sing. It impresses him like peaceful sounds from the hereafter, and yet he cannot face the procession. When it draws nearer, he steps aside and watches it move by from behind a dark bush that hides him from view. Alone, he weeps at the irretrievable loss he has suffered.

One sequence of scenes shows Faust on a sea voyage (II, 88-118). Always on the move and with no apparent goal, he has gone to sea in a flimsy boat that Mephistopheles had to produce for him. Faust expects the voyage to have a therapeutic effect: The uniformity of the sea will be more effective than the ever changing impressions on land in freeing him from oppression. During a storm, Faust throws the captain into the sea because he had shown fear and spoken about praying. The ship is wrecked. Faust and the rest of the crew are saved on an island and gather at an inn. Here Lenau juxtaposes the personality of one of the sailors, Görg, with that of Faust. Görg is a walking ideology rather than a real person. He represents a crass form of materialism. Cool and void of all feelings, he neither prays nor curses. He is indifferent to life and death and has no complaints when life seems to mishandle him. Conversely, he does not rejoice at times when others are happy. He likes wine and girls because, like fly swatters, they can be used to shoo away the minor irritations in life. When Faust asks him about his beliefs, Görg replies that he believes in what he sees, and nothing else. He does not believe in God or in His self-manifestation in the universe. Whatever Görg cannot understand, he rejects. When Mephistopheles approaches him, offering him his friendship, he will have nothing to do with him and dismisses him with an insult. Faust is greatly impressed with Görg's self-reliance and strength, but realizes all the more painfully that he is not made of the same stuff.

The last scene of the poem, "Fausts Tod" (II, 118-123), follows immediately after the Görg episode. Here Lenau tries to summarize the preceding events and, considering their lack of continuity, to assign them a function within the body of the work. In the end, Lenau leads the reader to the conclusion that the details of the external action were merely objective correlatives to the psychic development of Faust. His search has been aimless and has borne no fruit. He did not come to terms with life. Power and glory, which he did not seek to begin with, were futile. His moments of gross violence have alternated with spells of hopeless resignation and have merely hastened the disintegration of his soul. The narrow footbridge on which he had pictured himself at the beginning of the poem has become even more precarious and has now reached its end. The hereafter, in which he believes, signifies to him eternal damnation. Faust is at the point where he cannot live or die. There is no place for him in the universe. He illustrates the modern concept of the "unsheltered man" when he says:

Die Welle, die der Sturm bewegt,
Die schäumend an die Klippe schlägt,
Der Wind, der heulend Wälder splittert,
Der Blitz, der durch den Himmel zittert, –
Mehr Heimat haben sie und Ruh,
Mein einsam Herz, als du!

(II, 119)

("The storm-tossed wave pounding against a cliff, the roaring wind rending forests, the flash of lightning flickering through the sky – they have more of an abode and more peace than you, my forelorn heart.")

Faust meditates that the happiest man is he who slips directly from his mother's breast into the arm of death. Knowledge, even if it were accessible, would no longer satisfy him. He has but one desire now: "Könnt ich vergessen, daß ich Kreatur!" ("If I could only forget that I am a living entity" [II, 119]). Pursuing this trend of thought further, Faust, in the last few lines of the poem, makes an attempt to escape from his dilemma: He denies the reality of his own existence and that of the whole universe. The thought crosses his mind that there is no objective reality. The universe, the world, and man with his anxiety and his happiness are nothing but the dreams of a supreme being. Even the devil is now, to Faust, merely an insubstantial, dreamlike projection of God. There is no good and evil, no procreation and no murder.

Lenau's reduction of reality to God's dream and his notion that man, by virtue of being His dream, is directly part of Him, have led some critics to assert that Faust, and with him Lenau, sought rescue in pantheism. Such a conclusion is possible in terms of a logical derivation, but the immediate impact of Lenau's thoughts lies in an area other than theological speculation. They impress the reader first of all as outgrowths of a radical nihilism, and they bespeak archetypal despair.

In the end, Faust commits suicide. Having obliterated himself spiritually by denying his actual existence, he translates this idea into the physical realm and stabs himself to death. But even his death appears unreal to him, and he hopes to escape Mephistopheles by negating the reality of his death:

> Ich bin ein Traum mit Lust und Schuld und Schmerz,
> Und träume mir das Messer in das Herz!
>
> (II, 123)

("I am a dream with joy and guilt and pain, and I dream this knife into my heart.")

After searching for an identity and for his self, Faust has not only failed to find it, but has lost even the awareness of his physical existence and languidly drifts into an immaterial death. And yet his soul falls prey to the devil because his nonexistence was a piece of ephemeral self-deception. The poem, despite its artistic imperfections, comes close to being a direct transferral to art of an experience of life so hopeless and tormented that it touches on archetypal strata.

Faust was strangely received by Lenau's contemporaries. It is not surprising that the Young Germans and their followers, among them Gutzkow,[5] clamored against it. What is astonishing is the fact that those critics who praised it did so on religious grounds. The circle of the Swabian Poets welcomed it as the Christian answer to Goethe's supposedly pagan treatment of the theme. The circumstance that Lenau's Faust is not saved, as was Goethe's, gave rise to the somewhat unexpected conclusion that Lenau's work was much more Christian in spirit than Goethe's. Lenau did not record anywhere in writing his astonishment over this conclusion, but it must have been great. While working on *Faust,* he had never mentioned any religious intent, nor had he spoken of the alleged Christian character of the poem. Letters he wrote while working on *Faust* afford insights into his frame of mind at that time, of his intentions and expectations. Above all, they show that the figure of Mephistopheles fascinated him more than anything else. He said that he was writing the poem "from the heart of the devil" (III, 249), that he considered the subject-matter a suitable place to deposit all the "hellish stuff" (III, 243) that had accumulated in him, that the good-natured Swabians would be startled by the "genuine black devilish vein" (III, 263) threaded through the poem, and, finally, that Gustav Schwab, a trained theologian, would consider him an "arch-atheist" (III, 249) on account of the work. Yet many critics insisted on seeing in it what they were looking for, and *Faust* was cheered as a poetic manifestation of Christian orthodoxy.

The major critical evaluation was a monograph by a young Danish theologian, Hans Lassen Martensen (1808-1884), who later became an eminent professor of theology, court preacher, and Bishop Primate of the Danish Church. Having read Lenau's *Faust,* he called on the poet in Vienna while travelling in Central Europe. For the next two years, Martensen assumed the role of Lenau's spiritual mentor. According to Lenau, they sometimes discussed religious questions "from four to eight hours every day" (IV, 227). Under Martensen's guidance, Lenau tried to give a new direction to his life by embracing the authority of the Christian Church.

Martensen was a typical child of his age. He had arrived at his own religious philosophy, a kind of mystic-speculative eclecticism, by attempting to blend faith with reason, mystical intuition with critical speculation. He regarded all reflection as having its basis in the firm belief in God's absolute authority. Since man is God's creation, His authority is the *sine qua non* of man's thought. Therefore speculation is possible only on the basis of religious belief.[6] One of Martensen's students was Sören Kierkegaard who later violently turned against his teacher, and it was precisely the peculiar synthesis of belief and reason that provoked him.[7]

In his monograph, *Über Lenaus "Faust"* (Stuttgart, 1836), Martensen set out to prove that the poem was a glorification of theism and a deeply Christian treatment of the Faust theme. To a considerable extent he took Lenau's work merely as an excuse for expounding his own views: for example, that the period of philosophical and literary rationalism had finally come to an end, and that man's searching mind could find truth only in the belief in his Creator. The spirit of skepticism, he wrote, had to evolve further in one of two directions: It could surrender to, and be redeemed by, an unconditional belief in God, or it had to end in complete despair. Lenau's protagonist chose the latter course, and therefore, Martensen concluded with more zeal than acumen, the underlying philosophy of the work is proven to be deeply Christian. This interpretation is a good example of an *engagé* criticism that shirks the essential and belabors the irrelevant. Yet Lenau was deeply impressed by Martensen and eagerly accepted his praise as well as his further tutelage.

While befriending Martensen, Lenau wrote his *Savonarola* and, in 1840, published a revised version of *Faust,* with substantial additions. It is this version that is always read and appears in all editions of Lenau's works. The changes reflect Martensen's influence and show what Lenau must have intended to be a more solid philosophical-religious foundation for the poem. However, the impact which his *Faust* had in its original form is lost to a considerable extent. One possible reason that Lenau may have had for making the changes was that he felt that his poem ought to live up to what his readers said they saw in it. In a letter to Sophie he remarked that his changes were supposed to "clarify Faust's attitude toward the Christian religion" (IV, 399). In the version of 1840, Faust is no longer a confused self-seeker, but a dialectically thinking intellectual. What he struggles against is no longer an incomprehensible force deaf to the woes of man, but the Christian Church.[8]

Besides changes in the existing passages, a substantial scene was added in the second version: "Das Waldgespräch" (II, 83-87). It brings the total number of scenes to twenty-four. "Das Waldgespräch" is a versified piece of philosophy which takes the form of a dialogue between Faust and Mephistopheles. The abstract ideas in this scene were more important to Lenau than the characters who speak them. Some of the thoughts the devil mouths are entirely out of character. Instead of rejoicing, he is chagrined at the cleavage between man and nature. In a virtual lecture, he blames the Jewish religion for having brought about this split. The Indians and the Greeks had seen man and nature as a unity, but the Jews, he says, drove a wedge between the two. This wedge was their belief in a Messiah. Spinoza, he continues, attempted to mend the break, but to no avail. Nature was "betrayed" forever and has withdrawn from man.

Subsequently Mephistopheles reassumes his true role. When Faust asks what man should turn to, after having lost his belief in the Messiah as well as his bonds with nature, the devil replies that he will build for Faust a temple in which his own thought will be God (II, 86). Faust's separation from nature is complete. He is now bent on pursuing his ego, to "follow the path into his self" (II, 87). These thoughts, it has been shown, reflect the interpretation of the teachings of Kant and his followers as practiced in the first half of the nineteenth century.[9] Kant saw nature as a phenomenon and declared it to be the province of practical reason. Fichte's Transcendental Idealism showed man to be subject to neither the authority of religion nor the bonds of nature. Schelling's Nature Philosophy and Novalis' concept of Magic Idealism are part of this tradition, and Hegel's Panlogism is the final step in the development of post-Kantian subjectivism. Everything that exists—God and the world—is only a manifestation of man's reasoning power.

In the revised version, Faust's death acquires new connotations. Mephistopheles' triumph over him now points to the existence of a reality that reaches beyond the consciousness of the ego. The poem has now received a theoretical basis and signifies the collapse of the subjectivistic-idealistic philosophy. At the same time, the unity of the original work has suffered, for individuation, subjectivism, and insubordination toward the Church play only a limited part in the new version and are in conflict with Faust's otherwise nihilistic attitude. The original poem was more uniform. In the revised version Lenau introduced new ideas without being able to integrate them fully. The earlier Faust of 1836 reduced himself to nothingness out of his own choice and the needs of his self. The fate of the Faust of 1840, although it seems that he is punished for what he believed and did, is obscured by conflicting tendencies.

II Savonarola

Faust comes close to being Lenau's perfect self-portrayal. The nothingness into which his hero is driven at the end of the poem is a reflection of Lenau's own inner experiences. Yet the poet's fate was worse than that of his protagonist, for he constantly lived in the frame of mind that Faust reached only in the final scene. Nevertheless, after the appearance of *Faust,* Lenau's friends and friendly critics announced that the poem's hero was by no means a self-portrait of the poet. Faust's skepticism, they said, was not part of his creator's thinking. And there was a general anticipation that Lenau, now that he had written what they regarded as the denunciation of the negative philosophy, would soon write another large work affirming the positive one.

The variants in the second edition of *Faust* showed Lenau in the frame of mind in which he wrote his next long poem, *Savonarola,* with Martensen as a guiding star. In a letter to his mentor of July 14, 1836, Lenau speaks of his spiritual dependence on him, calling him his "invisible censor" (a strange term for Lenau to use, considering his protracted struggle against official censorship). Lenau wrote that his invisible censor hovered near him during his work, and that he often asked himself whether or not Martensen would approve of a given passage (IV, 234).

It is almost certain that Martensen influenced Lenau in the choice of themes for his next projected works: Huss, Savonarola, and Hutten. In a letter to Emilie Reinbeck, Lenau speaks of these projects as his "poetic assignment" (IV, 228). All three would deal with reformatory movements—an interesting choice for a Catholic poet. He turned to Savonarola as his first choice and began with the composition in the spring of 1836. The poem was finished within a year. The subject matter is fascinating and has often been treated by poets and writers, in the more recent past by Thomas Mann (*Gladius Dei,* 1902; *Fiorenza,* 1906).

Girolamo Savonarola (1452-1498) was a Dominican monk from Ferrara who devoted his life to the struggle for a reform of the Roman Catholic Church, especially the papacy. As prior of St. Mark's in Florence, he attacked the conditions at the court of Pope Alexander VI and appealed for a general Council. A powerful preacher, his popularity was so great that he became the law-giver of Florence after the downfall of the Medicis (1494) and for several years virtually ruled the city. Under the spell of Savonarola's magnetic presence, the Florentines abjured luxuries, dressed with Puritan plainness, and eagerly participated in the "religious carnivals" Savonarola staged repeatedly. In their course, they burned works of art and other "vanities." At the same time, Savonarola's attacks upon Pope Alexander grew so unrestrained that he was excommunicated. Eventually, the citizenry of Florence turned against him. He was arrested by the signory and put on trail. The Pope browbeat the city government into condemning him to death, and Savonarola was burned at the stake in 1498.

In writing his Savonarola poem, Lenau had no intention of presenting a historically accurate picture. Instead, he used the subject matter primarily as a vehicle for his own ideas, and as a platform in the controversies of the decade between the conservatives and the liberals, the theological orthodox and progressives, the defenders of Christendom and the advocates of pagan Hellenism, the late Romanticists and the Young Germans. Lenau's love for Sophie Löwenthal became another important factor in his approach to the theme. He and Sophie had had a serious disagreement in February, 1836. Sophie, a very devout woman despite her hysterical possessiveness, was eager to give their relationship religious overtones when they finally made peace. In a poem she sent to Lenau she stated that their love should thereafter be devoted to the principle of "struggling and renouncing cheerfully" (*freudig kämpfen und entsagen* [IV, 12]). Lenau bowed to her request, and his adoration of Sophie acquired strong religious overtones.

Lenau's main source for his *Savonarola* was Andreas Gottlob Rudelbach's *Hieronymus Savonarola und seine Zeit* (Hamburg, 1835; cf. VI, 100). Rudelbach was a friend and former teacher of Martensen. For several details Lenau used works by Karl Meier, Ludwig Flathe, and William Roscoe.[10] He proceeded, as he always did in his longer works, by beginning with those scenes that appealed to him especially, and arranging and connecting them later. The strophic form of the poem is that of the *Romanze*: four lines of iambic tetrameters. The rhyme scheme, a b a b, is more restrictive than that of "Klara Hebert," which was a b c b. Comprising nearly a thousand stanzas, the poem is subdivided into twenty-five episodes, each with a title. The episodic, stanzaic form of a longer narrative, widely used by the German Romanticists, had been introduced into German literature through Herder's translation of the Spanish *Poema del Cid* (1805). Friedrich de la Motte Fouqué and Clemens Brentano used the form, and so did several poets close to Lenau: Ludwig Uhland, Gustav Schwab, and Anastasius Grün, not to mention such poetasters among his friends and relatives as Max Löwenthal and Anton Schurz. In conformity with the form's requirements, Lenau singled out salient features, treated these in some detail, and disposed of all connecting events in a few lines at the beginning of each section. The lyric element is strong and outweighs the narrative in some of the episodes.

The disparate impulses from which Lenau's creative urge sprang in the composition of this work are not fully blended in the finished product. Least satisfactory are the opening scenes and the end. Here Lenau attempted to create the harmonious atmosphere of man living in the secure shelter of religion, but the devices he used were not adequate for his intentions. Savonarola's arrival at the Dominican monastery is a good example of the discrepancy between Lenau's goal and his vehicle. Depicting the world of peace inside the monastery walls, he used images that are clichés and do not penetrate to the layer of poetic truth.

The prior, ancient and white-haired, is shown in the monastery garden, watering flowers, his face illuminated by the sunset. He lectures to the young visitor on the analogy of flower life and monastic life. Flowers, he says, are chaste and pure, live, as by vows, in cheerful poverty. Obediently they rise from their beds when the hours of spring summon them and hurry to the great Mass to present an offering of fragrance. After the prior has finished speaking, a host of blossoms fall from a tree and descend upon his brow and hands, kissing them in gratitude (II, 139-140). These are, without a doubt, among the worst stanzas Lenau ever published. The diction is hackneyed, and the imagery reminiscent of the stylized landscapes of Hölty. One critic, otherwise a faithful admirer of Lenau, compared these scenes to certain cheap religious oil prints and justly dismissed them as "oleography."[11] The vain search by Savonarola's parents for the lost son (II, 132-138) belongs to this category, and so does the episode "Die Novizen" (II, 141-144), wherein Savonarola and another young monk, Domenico, establish a friendship that will last unto death. Only that friendship will never end, wrote Lenau, which is formed while two hearts, before the countenance of God, thrill with gladness over each other (II, 142). Absorbed in deep and silent contemplation, the two transport their souls into the realm of "holy darkness" (II, 143) where all of man's yearnings are fulfilled. Communication with God must be without words. Any sound would turn the friends' thoughts, like shy deer, away from the spring that is God. The prior eventually approaches them and leads them back to the more practical world of their daily duties.[12] The act of withdrawal within oneself, as here portrayed by Lenau, pertains to the world of religious mysticism, but the presentation does not live up to the poet's intentions.

Savonarola abounds with metaphors and similes. True, Lenau's poetic creativity expressed itself to a high degree through figures of speech, but here they occur in unusual concentration. Their function is almost purely decorative. Josef Nadler's harsh statement that Lenau's colorful imagery is "nothing but words"[13] does apply to portions of *Savonarola,* while it is unjust on the whole. The realm of oleography extends to a vision which Savonarola has after being tortured to confess (II, 255-260). Characteristically, he sees the image of his parents and his childhood. Together, they enter Paradise and are received by choirs of angels, patriarchs, prophets, apostles, anchorites, and martyrs. An angel assures Savonarola's mother that henceforth she will never be separated from her son; whereupon she joins the chorus. They all stroll through heavenly fields and orchards and watch the fish in a pond dance to their singing. As they approach God's throne, the atmosphere is filled with one great prayer. At this moment, Lenau has Savonarola wake up to the beat of his own heart.

Lenau's futile attempts to give poetic life to such scenes are not to be dismissed impatiently; they are poignant failures. The images of peace and a metaphysical abode that he tried to draw were meaningful to him mostly in the realm of his own existence. He wanted to find the rest and reconciliation which his hero found; and he hoped that by throwing himself into the arms of mysticism he would find his own salvation as well as a new purpose as an artist. Having tried to annihilate himself, physically and spiritually, in the guise of Faust and having hoped to enter the domain of non-existence, he now wanted to reach a realm of divine security in his *Savonarola.* The artisitc inadequacy of the above passages shows that his attempt was futile. After completing the poem, Lenau changed his viewpoint and turned away from mysticism.

If the quest for a mystic union with a supreme order and a supreme being was one salient feature of the poem, literary, socio-political, and theological polemics are equally important. Through his association with the members of the circle of Swabian Poets in Stuttgart, Lenau had come into conflict with the Young Germans, especially Ludwig Börne, Karl Gutzkow, and Heinrich Heine. Heine's association with the Young Germans was as loose as that between Lenau and the Swabian Poets. Heine and Lenau could not always hide their admiration for each other as poets. Each was thoroughly familiar with the work of the other and able to recite entire poems from memory. However, through their tenuous connections with groups whose most vocal members were the worst poets, they found themselves pitted against each other in their friends' altercations.

The first disparaging remarks about the Swabian Poets were made by Goethe in a letter to Karl Friedrich Zelter on October 4, 1831. He poked fun at Pfizer and Uhland and accused them of wrapping their shoddy artistry in a "moral-religious-poetic beggar's cloak, so that a showing elbow would have to be considered 'poetic intention' "[14] The letter appeared in print in 1834, and the Swabian Poets were deeply hurt. Heine followed suit by attacking the Swabians in his *Zur Geschichte der Religion und Philosophie in Deutschland* (1835) and in the third book of his *Romantische Schule* (early 1836), and Gutzkow in his *Beiträge zur Geschichte der neuesten Literatur* (1836). When Lenau's *Savonarola* appeared, the literary bickering was only at its beginning. A year later, in 1838, Pfizer published an essay, "Heines Schaffen und Tendenz" in the *Deutsche Vierteljahrsschrift*. Lenau wrote to his publisher, Cotta, that in this essay Pfizer had "brought Heine face to face with his own corpse" (VI, 18). The strife continued. In his *Romantische Schule,* Heine had ridiculed Uhland's poem "Der Schäfer." In 1838, Lenau replied with a parody of Goethe's "Schäfers Klagelied," entitled "Dichters Klagelied über das Junge Deutschland" (I, 496) and circulated it privately. In this parody he lamented the downfall of art in the new literary era and castigated the Young Germans in drastic terms. In 1839, Heine published his "Schwabenspiegel," another spoof on the Swabians, and in the same year Heine and Gutzkow attacked Karl Mayer in the *Jahrbuch der Literatur*. In 1843, Heine took the Swabians to task in *Atta Troll* (Chapter 22) with more humor than malice. Karl Mayer was his preferred whipping boy, but Mayer appreciated a good joke and was reportedly always the first to greet Heine's diatribes with laughter.[15] Not so Lenau. In one of his poetic replies to the Young Germans, entitled "An Karl Mayer" (I, 497), he consoled his friend: "As soon as you pluck a string, the dog [Heine] begins to howl." In another, "Die Frivolen" (I, 497), Lenau unleashed a singular barrage of abuse against writers who prostitute themselves. The allusions to Heine are thinly veiled. What speaks in Lenau's favor is the fact that he did not let these assaults appear in print.

Literary altercations were only part of the *engagement* with which Lenau approached the composition of his *Savonarola.* Theological disputes were of even greater importance, and Lenau's subject matter was germane to them. In 1835, the writings of Georg Hermes, professor of Catholic Theology at the University of Bonn, were banned by the pope, and the dissemination of his teachings was prohibited. Hermes had assigned reason, doubt, and intellect a central place in all theological investigation.

The ensuing "Hermesianic Controversy" was restricted to Catholic theology, to be sure, but similar attitudes prevailed in the Protestant camp and in contemporary intellectual life in general. Heine and David Friedrich Strauss were the champions of a rationalistic approach to religion which, in the case of Heine, borders on atheism. The appearance of Strauss' *Life of Jesus* in 1835 was the beginning of open warfare between the theological conservatives and progressives. The theologian Strauss recognized what he called the "philosophical wisdom" of the idea of Christianity, but he sharply questioned the authenticity of the Gospels and the historicity of Jesus. All religion was, to him, the product of a vast, myth-creating imagination, and the life of Jesus a fairy tale. The qualities and characteristics ascribed to Jesus, Strauss asserted, were not evoked by the concrete existence of one individual person; they were the products of what Carl Gustav Jung later would have called the "collective unconscious." Strauss' teachings were considered a threat in many quarters besides that of orthodox theology. The prospect of the destruction of Christian ideology made for strange bedfellows. Pietists and nationalistic fanatics, defenders of political absolutism and orthodox theologians, they all stood up against Strauss.

Heine went further than Strauss. In his *Zur Geschichte der Religion und Philosophie in Deutschland,* published in the same year as Strauss' work, he prophesied the imminent end of Christianity, calling it an ideology that would not be needed much longer. The essay runs precisely counter to what Novalis had demanded in his *Die Christenheit oder Europa* (1799): Christianity as the spiritual bond unifying the continent. Heine defined Christianity, divine and pure in its inception, as the religion of Spiritualism. But mankind had outgrown Spiritualism, he wrote, and the Christian ideology was now a remainder of humanity's adolescence. Modern man no longer yearns for the heavenly Host, but for bread. He is still weakened from the "holy vampires of the Middle Ages," and it will take time before "matter" is reinstituted into its rightful place that had been usurped by the "spirit" for so long. The senses, Heine demanded, must be re-established in their rightful respected place, and the physical cult and sensualism of Greek antiquity must be revived. Nine years before Nietzsche was born, Heine spoke of the death of the "old God": "Do you hear the bell? Kneel down. A dying God is given the last rites."[16] Heine, a resident of Paris, became identified with the tendencies of Saint-Simonism, a radical movement seeking social and political reform and guided by what its adherents regarded as the scientific laws of evolution. Young Germany became closely associated with Saint Simonism and with the Italian movement of radical politics, "La Giovine Italia," founded by Giuseppe Mazzini in 1830.

When Lenau prepared to enter the controversies of his time through the medium of his *Savonarola,* the two opposing camps were clearly defined. On the one side there were the defenders of the *ancien régime,* of religious orthodoxy, of biblical Christianity, the opponents of the "great pagan" Goethe, the conservatives, the Late Romanticists, the Spiritualists, and the "Nazarenes." Lenau sided with them. The other camp united the Young Germans, the modern literati, the political radicals, the innovators and liberals, the Hegelians, the religiously progressive and the Anti-Christians, the sensualists, the "Hellenists." Lenau depicted his protagonist as a champion of the Nazarenes, and the pope and his court as representatives of Hellenism. This is the basic distribution of forces in the poem. Savonarola's first sermon, delivered on a Christmas Eve, outlines his position and causes ill will at the papal court (II, 149-156).

In explaining the significance of Christmas (*Weihnacht*), Savonarola stresses the second part of the compound word: *Nacht* (night). He speaks of it in mystic and Romantic images. It is the time of introspection, he says, the time of contacts with an inner, unconscious life. Christmas is a mystery beyond man's comprehension and made possible through man's languishing desire for God, a desire that reaches heaven in the form of prayers. Savonarola advocates a personal, living God, and takes to task the pantheists and those who claim to perceive God in nature. With irony, he invites his listeners to go to Rome and witness the Christmas celebration there to see priests in rich garments absent-mindedly go through the motions of the ritual in desecrated churches. A thousand candles burn, but the hearts are cold. While celebrating Mass, priests ponder their next amorous adventure, plan a hunting trip, or imagine themselves in their favorite gambling house. Ceremony has become to them a meaningless gesture and caricature of what it is supposed to be. These particular reproaches were borrowed by Lenau from the writings of Luther. Likewise, the manner in which Savonarola receives his calling to the cloth in the midst of a storm is a detail that Lenau culled from the life of Luther rather than from that of Savonarola. Toward the end of his sermon, Savonarola prophesies a new golden age of Christendom, the purification of the Church, and the triumph of simple belief.

In the next scene, a papal emissary arrives in Florence: Mariano. His assignment is to defeat Savonarola in a public debate. In Lenau's poem, Mariano is the epitome of Hellenism and everything associated with it. In his sermon he quotes Cicero, Virgil, Plato, Aristotle, employs the rhetorical devices of classical antiquity, and mocks the prophets who would banish all joy. In a direct attack he names Savonarola as a purloiner of pleasure, a poisoner of the world, and a herald of misfortune (II, 159). He admonishes the people not to believe Savonarola, who sees misery everywhere, and not to fear that sensual pleasure might destroy their religious feelings. The sermon ends in an apotheosis of the ruler of Florence, Lorenzo de' Medici, his splendid power, and the renaissance of the spirit of classical antiquity that flourishes under his supremacy.

Savonarola's reply follows in the subsequent section. Calling Mariano a "comedian in the pulpit" (*Kanzelgaukler* II, 166), he accuses him of insincerity. With his soothing oratory, he says, Mariano dulls the "sacred dolor" of man: His "classical prattle" does nothing to strengthen man's belief. Savonarola attacks viewpoints that Mariano, in the context of Lenau's work, had never expressed, but which are familiar from Strauss' writings: Christ, Savonarola maintains, is not an idea, not the sum of the divine thoughts conceived by men. God in human form, the *Gottmensch*, did live. Here Lenau's protagonist is refuting ideas from Strauss' *Life of Jesus* that have nothing to do with the historical Savonarola and his adversaries. The Florentine monk merely assailed conditions at the papal court, and never challenged the doctrine of the Church.

From Strauss and Heine, Lenau proceeded to Hegel. He introduced Savonarola's brief attack on him with the phrase:

"In a coming age, some fools will say . . ." (II, 169). Savonarola's easy prophecy is concerned with Hegel's concept that God is identical with man's idea of Him. God does not emerge in man, Savonarola argues, but man may embrace God as a guest from heaven. The mystical inclinations of Lenau's hero do not apply to the historical Savonarola either. When Lenau's Savonarola exclaims that prayer is identical with man's cognition of God, the poet gave voice to a mystical sentiment foreign to the historical Florentine monk.

In Lenau's poem it is never decided whether Savonarola or Mariano won the oratory contest. It was Lenau's intention to have his protagonist triumph over the papal emissary, but most readers feel that Mariano's sermon is more inspired than Savonarola's. This is quite true. Mariano speaks with ease and elegance and draws a glowing picture of a world in which art rules supreme. In contrast, Savonarola is a "gloomy, headstrong ascetic," (II, 159), his sermon has a dull ring, and in his presentation he is hampered by Lenau's insistence on having him discuss mostly theoretical issues. One cannot help concluding that Lenau subconsciously felt more enthusiasm for the cause of Mariano than for that of Savonarola. Lenau became aware of this inconsistency after the poem had appeared in print. In 1838 he sent a copy to Emilie von Gleichen-Russwurm, Schiller's daughter, and asked her to judge for herself whether or not the reproach that Mariano defends pagnism better than Savonarola upholds Christianity was justified. "I did not intend to do this," he wrote, "but the poet is excused, for he does not at all times have control over his inner voice" (IV, 285).

Lenau depicts the doings of Savonarola's antagonists with obvious relish. He describes at length scenes from life among the Borgias in Rome, their conspiracies, intrigues, and murders. The two sons of Pope Alexander VI entertain incestuous love affairs with their sister, Lucrezia, and so does her father. During an orgy, one of the brothers, Cardinal Cesare Borgia, is seized by jealousy and arranges for the murder of the other, the Prince of Gandia. His body is fished from the Tiber River the morning after. In a conversation with his father (toward whom he harbors thoughts of patricide), Cesare readily admits having masterminded his brother's murder and prides himself on his indifference toward divine justice. He says that his religious disbelief matches that of his father (II, 208-220).

In the grossness of these scenes, coolly presented in the even gait of the four-line stanza of the *Romanze,* Lenau at times transgressed the bounderies of good taste. He is dangerously close to achieving unwanted comical effects. Yet the high pitch exhibited here is characteristic of many portions of the poem. The jarring dissonance between these parts and others that evoke an atmosphere of quiet introspection is another unsolved conflict within the poem and contributes to its lack of unity.

Most remarkable is the presence of the same high pitch in passages concerning Savonarola. Not everything connected with the positive Christian cause is presented in the benign, at times artificial, tone discussed above. The outstanding characteristics of Lenau's protagonist are intensity and fanaticism. He does not impress the reader as an actual person, but as the embodiment of an idea. His character is not fully shown. It has been said that Lenau's Savonarola resembles figures in children's puppet theaters. They are shown with a certain expression which they maintain throughout the action, no matter how inappropriate this expression may be at times.[17]

Savonarola's concept of Christianity, which—in Lenau's eyes—runs contrary to that of the rationalistic, pleasure-seeking papal court, dwells intensely on pain, mental torment, and death. In his dispute against Mariano the reformer explains that there is a wound burning in man's heart and that Mariano is trying to veil and conceal it. But "Die Wunde läßt sich nicht verschleiern, / Ihr Blut durchdringt den dünnen Flor" ("The wound cannot be veiled; the blood penetrates the thin gauze" [II, 167]).

In the context of the poem, the significance of the wound is never explained. We are merely told that the only remedy for it is the love inherent in the Christian gospels. The metaphor of the wound is, in the end, more applicable to Lenau than to his subject-matter. It bears a strong resemblance to other predominant images in which Lenau had expressed his despair, and the quoted lines contain the same metaphor Lenau had used in his dejected attempt to characterize the nature of his work: bloodstained tatters of an inadequate dressing. To Savonarola, suffering is the central experience in man's life:

In dieses Lebens Kampfgewühlen
Bis an des Friedens Morgenrot
Ist *Schmerz* noch unser tiefstes Fühlen,
Der innerste Gedanke – *Tod.*

(II, 172)

("In the battle tumult of this life, to the dawn of final peace, pain is our profoundest sensation, and death our most intimate thought.")

He says that God, in order not to forsake us, took the same pain upon Himself through the act of His crucifixion, and thus made Christianity a religion of suffering. In one scene of allegorical significance, Leonardo and Michelangelo spend a night in the gardens of the Medicis in order to contemplate the classical works of art that adorn them (II, 224-227). At the same time, the plague is raging in Florence, and while the two artists admire the serene image of Apollo, a funeral procession is moving past outside the garden. The wild lamentations of the poor who go to bury their dead can be heard from afar. The artists, embittered by this experience, renounce the forms of classicism which can no longer convey their creative impulses. They turn to the world of Christian art which appears, by contrast, unbridled and conditioned by torment and holy fervor. Through the experience of pain, Michelangelo exclaims, the "profound world of Christian art" has unfolded before his eyes. At this moment, Leonardo conceives of the idea for his Last Supper, and Michelangelo—called "the wild one" by Lenau—is entranced and frightened by a concept for a piece of sculpture, the Deposition from the Cross.

In his sermon to the dying Lorenzo, Savonarola dwells on the same juxtaposition of Christianity and paganism. "God has become identical with pain" (II, 176), he tells the ruler, and reminds him that not even the great of this world can escape the experience of torment (II, 183). Lorenzo, the great patron of classicism, has to hear that the lovely dream in which the ancient people indulge is too shallow for modern man. The wisdom of the Greeks cannot cover the deep "rupture" in man's heart (II, 184). Their art shunned the abyss of pain (II, 185). But now, Savonarola exclaims, twilight has set in, the world has learned to think profoundly, "the abyss gapes, the Savior calls; the gay delusions and the multitude of pagan gods disperse in the wind" (II, 185). The images of the abyss and the wound or ruptured heart are among Lenau's most frequent and genuine. While he saw in religion a strikingly modern therapeutic device that was meant to redeem him from the oppression of his psyche, he also ascribed to it the very characteristics of the despair that beset him.

Savonarola is associated not only with images of torment, but also with those of its psychological complement: violence.

In this respect he resembles Ziska and, to some extent, Faust. Savonarola is made God's warrior through a flash of lightning (II, 137); his words gather a thousand flashes of lightning into a rod of fire to scourge the sinners (II, 146). One great desire "burns throughout" his life (II, 144): to purge the Church. Commenting on the outbreak of the plague in Florence, Lenau indirectly compares the epidemic to Savonarola and calls it "the other admonisher who speaks in a sharper idiom" (II, 221). Savonarola rejects the offer of a cardinal's hat and replies to a messenger of Pope Alexander that he wants to win only one red hat—one that is dyed in his own blood (II, 205). His ecstatic death on the pyre symbolically sums up his fiery life. Ferocity also abounds in scenes not centered around the hero: in the characterization of Tubal; in the description of the frenzied love orgies at Alexander's court; and in a savage battle scene in San Marco, Savonarola's monastery. The preponderence of ferociousness and even sadism in a religious poem has offended many readers. The Viennese writer and physician Ernst von Feuchtersleben, a friend and otherwise an admirer of Lenau, wrote in his *Confessionen*:

> A certain intolerant, monkish vandalism is distasteful to the serene reader, especially if he loves art and life. And the lyrical chirping of blossoms, springs, bushes, etc. in the most serious moments is truly annoying to the sensitive reader.[18]

The reception of *Savonarola* was as mixed as that of *Faust*. What could not have been an altogether welcome praise came from Wolfgang Menzel, the vociferous propagator of a narrow form of patriotism. In his *Literaturblatt*,[19] he declared Lenau a fellow fighter for the cause of German nationalism and used the poem as a buttress in one of his diatribes against his archenemy, Heinrich Heine. Journals of the opposite camp took up the challenge, for example Gutzkow's *Telegraph für Deutschland*,[20] and attacked Lenau together with Menzel. It is true that Lenau had provided Menzel with fuel, but he did not like being drawn into his particular brand of squabble. Lenau vented his anger in a (published) epigram directed at Menzel, entitled "Einem unberufenen Lober" (I, 503), asking him not to soil with sticky sweet approbation the rim of the inspired cup that he, the poet, is draining already, without Menzel's encouragement. Menzel's revenge was forthcoming. In his literary history of Germany he treated Lenau most unkindly and disposed of *Savonar-*

ola with one sour sentence.[21] Another uncalled-for eulogizer was an aspiring poet by the name of Uffo Horn, who wrote an acclamatory monograph on Lenau's poem,[22] praising it with such lack of moderation that the harm he did exceeded the good. Martensen had careful words of approbation.[23] He liked the poet's Christian attitude and mystical inclinations, but not the infusion of political matter and the intemperate invectives against the Hegelians and other progressives.

The bickering that followed the appearance of *Savonarola*, in addition to rousing the attention of the bureau of censorship, was partly responsible for the poet's sudden weariness of his protagonist and everything he stood for. His religious and philosophical outlook had shifted when he set out on his next long poem, *Die Albigenser*.

CHAPTER 7

Last Ecstasies: The Albigenses and Don Juan

I Die Albigenser

AFTER completing his *Savonarola,* Lenau embarked on the second part of his projected trilogy, the part concerned with Huss and the Hussite Wars. He studied sources extensively. In a letter to Max Löwenthal, he gave an interesting reason for finding his new subject-matter so attractive. He wrote that he would like to give voice to the "wild spirits" within him which "had to be restrained for so long" during the composition of *Savonarola* (IV, 257). Apparently Lenau himself was no longer aware of the ferocious, predatory aspects of his most recent work and considered it, in retrospect, a meek and gentle poem that had necessitated a curbing of his true nature. But he soon found that the new subject-matter was not sufficiently interesting and diversified for his purposes, and he contented himself with a short cycle on one towering figure in the Hussite Wars, Ziska (cf. Chapter 5). Yet the theme of reformatory movements and religious wars continued to exercise its magic upon Lenau. Late in 1837 he chanced upon works on the Albigensian Wars, a number of punitive campaigns in the nature of crusades led by the Church against heretic sects in Southern France in the thirteenth century. He had found what he wanted: a vehicle for giving free rein to his "wild spirits."

The name "Albigenses" is derived from the town of Albi near Toulouse in southern France and designates a variety of sects flourishing in that vicinity. It is difficult to find a common denominator for the various doctrines of the Albigenses. They were essentially Catharists and Manichaean Dualists[1] who believed in the existence of two eternal principles or gods, one good and one evil. In this world they saw the true purgatory or hell, and in man the result of a contention between the two principles. At death, man is recreated in a similar or lower form of life and has to dwell in this world unless he dies reconciled to God through Christ.

Information concerning the details of the Albigenses' beliefs is not always reliable, since it was transmitted through the writings of members of the Roman Church only. All Albigenses shared one thing: their strong opposition to the Roman Church. They denied the resurrection of the body and the immortality of the soul, did not recognize the seven sacraments and the Old Testament, referred to the Catholic Church as the abode of the evil principle, and called the pope the Antichrist. They first appeared in southern France early in the eleventh century and gained ground under the protection of the Dukes of Aquitaine. The Roman Church was unable to persuade the local secular authorities to eradicate the heresy. The movement spread until Pope Innocent III, impatient at the failure of his attempts at a peaceful conversion, called for a crusade (1209). The war that followed lasted for twenty years, was waged with the utmost savagery on both sides, and destroyed the Provençal civilization. What was left of the heretical spirit after the Treaty of Paris (1229) was quelled by the Inquisition during the next century.

Lenau's choice of subject-matter horrified all those who had admired his *Savonarola.* It became apparent that he was no longer in the same frame of mind in which he had written the previous poem. He took great pains to dissociate himself from his former attitude and told Max Löwenthal that he could not understand how he could ever have written his *Savonarola.*[2] In November, 1839, he wrote a letter to Hermann Marggraff, a journalist and biographer who was collecting data on him. Lenau made a special point of distancing himself from mysticism, explaining that its presence in *Savonarola* was due to the subject-matter, not to the poet. "I consider mysticism a disease," he wrote (IV, 345). He assured Marggraff that he had not written his latest poem in order to present "an anti-Hegelian Christology in iambic verse." Making light of his attacks upon the Hegelian school, he shrugged them off as a "pruritus ingenii" —a mental itch.

In the same letter, he set himself apart from Wolfgang Menzel, averring that he was in no way close to him, did not want to be considered his "versifying shield bearer" (an accusation levelled by Gutzkow), and assured Marggraff that he had written his works without Menzel's advice and knowledge. Lenau found it more difficult to break the news of his changed outlook to Martensen, to whom he had dedicated the first edition of

Savonarola (but not the almost identical second one of 1844). In a letter of April, 1838, he wrote that he was suffering under a great mental depression due to the fact that the philosophy depicted in his poem had not yet worked to quiet and exalt him, the poet. He admitted that in unfortunate moments he felt tempted to question the cause of God, said that he realized the frivolity of such thoughts but could not help that his great sensitivity allowed such fumes to rise in his head. It may take some time, he confessed, hiding his embarrassment behind a high-flown metaphor, "behind a fresh breeze from the holy mountains will blow away my cap of mist" (IV, 274). Martensen was bitterly disappointed with his former disciple and deplored Lenau's development after *Savonarola.* The two never saw each other again, nor did they exchange any more letters.

On the surface, Lenau's *Die Albigenser* bespeaks a theological and philosophical outlook almost contrary to that found in *Savonarola.* From the beginning, Lenau had named "doubt" as the true hero of the work (IV, 344), and had set out to negate the positive attitude toward religion that he had adopted in his preceding poem. Yet in respect to poetic ideas and the creative impulse behind the subject-matter, the two poems are closely related. What attracted Lenau to both themes was the violence inherent in the revolts. The non-violent, ambrosial elements in *Savonarola* were not genuinely perceived by the poet. The structure of the various components in *Die Albigenser* presents a similar picture.

Lenau's main source was Friedrich Hurter's four volume *Geschichte Papst Innozenz des Dritten und seiner Zeitgenossen,* Hamburg, 1834.[3] He began his research in November, 1837, and the composition of the poem in the following summer. Initially, he envisaged the new work as a vast historical panorama and wrote the first few scenes with great enthusiasm. But soon the pace slowed down. His engagement to Karoline Unger and its termination, as well as the endless quarrels with Sophie during the following year, greatly hampered the progress of the poem. Moreover, Lenau's health failed repeatedly—unmistakable harbingers of the paretic collapse that was only five years off. As nearly as November, 1839, he told Max Löwenthal that all the joy in the writing of the poem had gone. The Albigenses and their "endless priestly atrocities" disgusted him, he said, and swore that the devil should fetch him if he ever ventured on another theological poem.[4] A few months later he realized that he would not be able to "round out the poem into a uniform whole" (IV, 179).

Late in 1840, he began to read in some of Hegel's works. From then on, he spoke enthusiastically of the philosopher and said that "mankind can be freed only along the path that Hegel cleared."[5] While Lenau was finishing *Die Albigenser*, Hegel's philosophy played the same role for him as Martensen's tutelage had played while he worked on *Savonarola*. Hegelian ideas do not appear, however, until late in the poem, since he had already worked on it for two years before reading Hegel. By the spring of 1841, he had lost all patience with the poem. He wrote to Sophie and Max that he merely wanted to finish it off, no matter how (V, 41). During the winter of 1841-2, reluctant to hand the manuscript over to his publisher, he made final revisions. In the summer of 1842, the poem went to press. While reading proof, Lenau realized that there was little connection among some of the scenes and that parts of the action remained unclear. He repaired some of the faults and tried to "introduce in the most disparate stretches the continuum which a book, after all, must have" (V, 93). The poem was ready for the autumn book fair of 1842. Contrary to Lenau's fears, no difficulties with the bureau of censorship resulted from its publication.

The work, subtitled "Freie Dichtungen," is subdivided into thirty-two episodes, each identified by a title. His choice of verse form was most fortunate. He broke away from the four-line stanzas employed in *Savonarola* and arranged each episode in blocks of lines of varying lengths. The meter is mostly iambic pentameter; the rhyme schemes vary. In comparison with his earlier epic poems, Lenau's language in *Die Albigenser* has become terser and more powerful. The poem is difficult, and at times it is hard to decide whether the difficulty is inherent in the matter or due to Lenau's insufficient control of it. The episodic structure, Lenau's accustomed form in his longer works, provided many pitfalls in this instance. Unable always to put himself into the mind of his reader, the poet overlooked the fact that the scores of names and events that he knew so well from his sources were not generally familiar. He closely followed details that interested him, without properly introducing and connecting them. In his panoramic view of events, he often touched on persons and events without returning to them, whirling the reader along in an endless kaleidoscope of horrors. This effect was surely in part intended, but, at the same time, the reader feels at a loss when faced with a confusing array of names and personages that he has no opportunity to get to know.

Many of the individual episodes are boldly drawn and rich in color, while in others the diction does not live up to the degree of violence Lenau sought to convey. A state of violent ecstasy is the common denominator of the poem. The first episode, "Nachtgesang" (II, 278-283), is an appeal by the poet to the allegorical figure of the tiger. He would like to have the tiger as a companion not only in his private life, to ward off his enemies, but also to give a destructive power to his verse. The poet is eager to conjure up the tiger's spirit and to see the animal as a projection of himself. It performs for him what he cannot do but wishes he could do: rout earthly desires and murder painful recollections. Above all, the image of a woman should be torn asunder and devoured. The tiger should help with his claws when the poet speaks out against tyrants. In great detail, Lenau depicts an imaginary scene in which the tiger attacks and dismembers a tyrant in his bed, tearing away at his entrails. In the end, the poet feels at one with the tiger:

> Schon ist in meinem Geist sein Hauch zu spüren
> Und durch mein Herz sein wildes Blut ergossen!
> (II, 280)

("Already I can feel its breath in my mind and its wild blood in my heart.")

As always when Lenau resorts to images of boundless violence, there is an element of impotence lurking behind his spasmodic identification with the tiger. The ecstasy is a wishful pose, and the poet can rarely live up to it. Psychologically, it is the complement of the inertia and static despair that Lenau experienced and evoked so genuinely. Like the Ziska cycle, *Die Albigenser* exhibits paroxysms of violence that have a marked pathological undertone. This can be illustrated in many ways. At the sight of the dead on a battlefield, a survivor asks himself about the eschatological basis of such slaughter and wonders if God might be a patient plagued by a fever, creating a world in moments of a hectic flush, and destroying it again in the seizure of a chill. He asks: "Is world history merely His freezing and burning?" (II, 340) Here Lenau clothed his own genuine experience of a desperate vacillation in a cosmic, quasi-religious image. His God is not dead but, more pathetically, infirm. The image closely resembles one familiar from *Faust*: God whirling a burning world around Himself to ward off boredom, as the shepherd whirls a firebrand at night to frighten off owls (II, 102). Both images are grandiose representations of Lenau's genuine inner experiences.

Although it was the "never ceasing battle din" that had caused Lenau to turn away from the Hussite Wars, his new poem proved to be an endless string of gory battle scenes and other forms of carnage. An episode depicting Pope Innocent kneeling in prayer before a cross underscores the fact that blind ferocity, more than anything else, is the poetic idea behind the work. The Pope kisses Christ's wounds, Lenau says, as a tame lion would lick his master's hand. But when Innocent tastes the blood of his master, his fury is unleashed and his fervent prayer turns into an attack upon what he worships:

> Er hat sein Bild schon halb zerrissen
> Und meint, es immer noch zu küssen.
> (II, 338)

("He has torn His image almost to shreds, and imagines that he is still kissing it.")

The image ties in with the motif of love and violence and also shows that in Lenau's eyes there was no rational cause for the Albigensian Wars. Once the fury is unleashed, it no longer matters against whom it is directed; it may even be against that which one loves most. The scene sets the pattern for the entire poem and evokes apocalyptic connotations.

Yet in the depths of Lenau's phyche, cruelty was not a primary emotion, but a compensation. Lenau's rendition of the fate of Fulco, the troubadour, illustrates this well (II, 295-306). The episode is based on the life of Folquet of Marseilles, one of the greatest Medieval troubadours (died 1231), consigned by Dante as a "bright jewel" to Venus, the third heaven, among the blessed spirits. For fifteen years, in his songs, Folquet celebrated Adalasia or Adelheid (the sources differ), wife of Barral, Viscount of Marseilles. Later he renounced the world, became a monk, and, in 1206, Bishop of Toulouse. In this capacity he urged Pope Innocent to suppress the Albigensian sects. He was most ruthless in his persecution of heretics and, according to one of the sources known to Lenau,[6] was directly responsible for some five hundred thousand deaths. Notwithstanding the fact that Folquet was on the side of the Roman Catholic Church and

Lenau's sympathies were with the Albigenses, he identified himself with him. In describing Fulco (he was a Genoese, and Lenau used the Italian form of the name) and his unfulfilled love for Adelheid, Lenau's own relationship to Sophie was foremost in his mind. Intensifying the situation, he lets Barral expel Fulco from his court in a fit of jealousy, and has Adelheid die subsequently. The description of Adelheid is a troubadour's song in itself, except that Fulco urges her to throw her sense of duty to the winds and love him. Fulco's final parting from Adelheid, as she lies in state, is described effectively. When the priests fear that Fulco might throw himself over her corpse and kiss it, he merely seizes from her hands the cross she is holding and presses it wildly against his lips. "Von Adelheidens Totenbahr / Riß ihn der Wahnsinn zum Altar" ("From Adelheid's bier, insane fury tore him away to the altar" [II, 305]).

After he takes the cloth, he "depicts hell with the same passion with which he praised the image of the woman" (II, 297). Lenau's additions to the source material throw an interesting light on his intentions. Not only did he relate the theme to his own experiences, but he connected closely the emotions of love and violence—an association that appears frequently in his later works. It appears in a note to Sophie written while he studied sources for *Die Albigenser*. Replying to Sophie's statement that he was fatefully and inexorably hers ("du bist mir verfallen"), Lenau wrote that he considered her his prey, too, and referred to himself as a vulture carrying her in his claws (IV, 129). The tiger's ferocity that he claimed for himself when working on the poem was, in part, sublimated eroticism. In a telling analogy, Lenau established a link between love and savagery. Some soldiers, not satisfied with having dealt their enemies mortal blows, pierce their corpses with their swords in the same manner as passionate love, "after having satisfied itself, continues, with drunken lips, to revel in kisses" (II, 365).

In presenting the details of warfare, Lenau was impartial. Both parties committed ghastly deeds and Lenau—perhaps out of a sense of fairness but more likely in fascination with the horrors—did not palliate the excesses of either. In painful detail he depicts scenes of such diabolical cruelty that he comes close to the grotesque at times. From his sources, he deliberately culled passages that offered him the possibility of giving free rein to his "wild spirits." In the scene entitled "Der Rosenkranz" (II, 331-338), the crusaders, led by an abbot and a military commander, Count Simon Montfort, storm a castle held by heretics. After taking it, Simon gives orders to have all survivors except one hundred killed. Then he has the hundred blinded except Hugo von Alfar, their leader; he is deprived of only one eye. They are told to hold on to a long rope and, led by the one-eyed knight, are despatched to Count Foix, one of the Albigensian leaders, as a living rosary. He is told to use it in his prayers of penance.

The counter blow is quickly forthcoming. During an unsuccessful siege of Carcassone, Foix has scores of crusaders killed while scaling the walls. Their corpses are bundled together into sheaves and thrown over the battlements as a greeting to Simon (II, 364). Mass killings are carried out for their own sake. When a city is taken, the abbot leading the crusaders urges them to kill everyone in sight, although there are many Catholics among them. "Even though they lie mixed up," he tells the soldiers, "the Dear Lord will pick out those that are His" (II, 366). There is a scene ("Foix," II, 359-362) where a heretic and his friends desecrate a church and celebrate a black mass, using religious imagery for profane purposes such as wenching and carousing; and another ("Der Büßer," II, 352-356) where Raymond Roger, Viscount of Beziers, has to do public penance. In one hand an abbot holds a stole that is tied around Raymond's neck and flagellates him with the other.

The imagery serves well to underscore the action. The word "blood" and its compounds occurs about fifty times in the 122 pages of the poem. In one battle scene, the spilled blood is so copious that the ground will no longer absorb it. A red lake fills the valley. In an allegorical image, war is pictured as a figure raging through the land (here referred to altogether as a "red puddle") with the red sky pulled over his head like a scarlet-red cap. Crusaders hurled off the walls of Carcassone are referred to as a "rain of corpses." Since others are still scaling the walls while their predecessors fall, Lenau perceives the scene as a permanent motion of rising and descending waters of a fountain (II, 363). The image well conveys the vastness and perpetuity of the death experience Lenau was trying to recreate.

Imagery concerned with exotic creatures abounds. In the words of a heretic, the Roman Church appears as a vengeful goddess armed with sword, trident, and blood-bucket, snakes coiled around her body.[7] Riding across the lands, she drops a snake here and there. The snakes turn into pestilence, starvation, war, and "clerical deceit" (II, 321). A monk who is forced to listen helplessly to a heretic's sermon sheds tears of wrath which turn into a dragon much more fearful than the snakes of the goddess Amadurga. The dragon is the Inquisition.

Interspersed among battle scenes are several short lyrical and contemplative pieces, small episodes of little consequence to the historical panorama, but of human significance. "Das Mädchen von Lavaur" (II, 370-372) concerns a young girl who is presumed dead and prepared for burial. She awakens a few days later after the city has been sacked and all its inhabitants killed. Realizing that she is the only survivor, she loses her mind. This scene, not contained in any of Lenau's sources, sprang from the poet's imaginiation. The same is true for "Jacques" (II, 345-347), the story of an insane tailor obsessed with the thought that the Antichrist cannot be buried unless he has a burial gown. Walking among dead soldiers, Jacques collects material for a gown large enough for the Antichrist. He dies after having finished one huge sleeve.

The theological side of the theme is treated in a number of episodes, without being fully integrated into the poem. Lenau drew some of the ideas directly from his sources; he transformed others to bring them into line with Hegel's teachings.

A good example of Lenau's inclination to introduce modern allusions in his poem is the scene "Das Gelage" (II, 379-382). Students in a Paris tavern are discussing philosophical and theological questions. They are followers of Amalric of Bena, a heretic among the professors of theology at the university. The historical Amalric (died c.1204) was the most radical of the heretics, so much so that his doctrines were designated as mental aberrations rather than heresy at the Lateran Council of 1215. Nevertheless, his followers were burned at the stake, and so was his exhumed body. A mystic pantheist, Amalric regarded everything, even the human body, as God and asserted that his followers could commit no sin. The group was notorious for its debaucheries.

Amalric's followers denied the existence of a hereafter, but believed that God manifested Himself in a threefold evolution: in Abraham, marking the epoch of the Father, or the Old Testament; in Jesus, who signified the epoch of the Son, or the New Testament; and in the era of the Holy Ghost, inaugurated by Amalric and his disciples. Lenau blended this dogma with Hegel's doctrine that the *Geist* realizes itself in three stages of development: the subjective, the objective, and the absolute. In fact, the two theories share the same basic pattern. What Lenau quotes as Amalric's teachings is actually a mixture of Amalric and Hegel's *Philosophy of Religion.* The Holy Trinity, one character says, is merely a metaphor for the three epochs of man's attempts to recognize God. Then follows a discussion of the three stages, culminating in the concept of God as *Geist.* At the end of the scene, the students shout, "Der Geist ist Gott" (II, 382). Lenau made good use of the fact that the term *Geist* is employed in German both in the theological sense of "Holy Ghost" and in Hegel's philosophical context.

When Lenau glorified the doctrines of Amalric, including his deification of the body, he had entirely abandoned the spiritual camp of Savonarola to join that of the martyr's adversary, Mariano. In 1838, he had suggested to Martensen—with an eye on Heine and his followers—the founding of a periodical that would combat "the ever noisier Messianic hymn of the flesh" (IV, 275). Four years later, he had practically joined forces with Heine who, in his *Zur Geschichte der Religion und Philosophie in Deutschland,* had advocated a new religion of the senses. He followed Heine's observation that people, in pursuing their Christian calling, had slaughtered each other for many centuries. "Christ? A curious fairy tale," Lenau wrote in his poem. "This dead mass of two armies, where everyone was killed in the delusion of his Christian duty, does not bespeak Christ's concern for us" (II, 340).

Hegel became Lenau's guiding star in the last phase of his work on *Die Albigenser.* Lenau discovered in Hegel's philosophy something he had never before experienced, namely, direction and purpose. By reconciling the finished sections of his work with Hegelian ideas, he tried to lend a positive significance to *Die Albigenser.* Not only in the theological portions of the poem, but also in his attempts to discover reason behind the slaughter that he had presented, Lenau brought Hegel's philosophy to bear. Hegel's doctrine of the irrepressible evolvement of the "Geist" applies not only to religion and art, but also to history. Hegel said that the course of world history moves along meaningful, rational lines and that, in fact, reason rules the world. World history, according to Hegel, is determined by the principle of eternal wisdom and constitutes progress in the realization of spiritual freedom. The evolvement of the spirit is not possible without human passions clashing in severe conflicts. Without crimes and suffering, Hegel held, no worthwhile accomplishments are possible. They are the tools of the universal spirit ("Weltgeist") in bringing about its own realization. Although history may, at times, cause the world to appear like a slaughterhouse, the development of the principle of the spirit is the true theodicy, for it hinges on the belief that even the smallest detail in the historical process is not only condoned by God, but is, in fact, His work.[8]

Lenau eagerly incorporated these thoughts into his poem in order to give his presentation meaning and purpose. He tried to show that even such conflicts as the Albigensian Wars were necessary and had their rightful place in history. Interspersing the action with references from Hegel, Lenau tries to interpret the war as a manifestation of the *Geist*. A supreme spirit directs the course of the war. At times it meditates in quiet self-absorption; then the warriors lie prostrate, and the battle subsides. At other times the spirit flares up brightly, as does the struggle (II, 393). Following Hegel, Lenau saw nature struggle toward light and freedom, "even though horror, pain, and death swarm up from under nature's holy feet" (II, 282).

Lenau eagerly utilized Hegel's defense of warfare, especially as presented in his *Philosophy of Right*. War, Hegel said, functions as a rejuvenator and innovator, and prevents the stagnation of mankind. In time of peace, Hegel wrote, the particularization of the individual goes unchecked and would eventually bring about the disintegration of the human race. War strengthens mankind and re-establishes the unity of those nations that have disintegrated within themselves in long periods of peace. The insecurity that war brings about—one must keep in mind that the frame of reference of even so abstract a thinker as Hegel was rooted in his time, and that war, to him, meant "hussars with drawn swords"[9]—is nothing more than the external commotion that is needed to effect the spiritual goal. These views are echoed in *Die Albigenser*. "The world is in need of arms" (II, 282), Lenau exclaims. Since the death of Jesus did not bring about a change in man, God must manifest Himself through another sacrificial death—death on the battlefield. The *Geist* must use sword and fire. If mankind is not to rot, Lenau said in a mixed metaphor, "the old wound must burst into flame again" (II, 283). These thoughts, except the image of the "old wound," are expropriated from Hegel. That image is, characteristically, Lenau's own.

In a further attempt to lend unity to the poem, Lenau viewed the Albigensian War as the earliest manifestation of the ceaseless quest for freedom. This aspect of the work, to be sure, was an after-thought, even more so than the sprinkling of the poem with Hegelian ideas. In an epilogue ("Schlußgesang," II, 398-400), Lenau points to the universality of the revolt he has described, and to its applicability to areas other than religion.

In a letter of October, 1841, Lenau wrote that he was adding the epilogue in order to make the poem more easily comprehensible to "less versatile readers" (V, 74). But even the most versatile reader would not have been able to draw from the body of the work what Lenau "summarized" in the end. Because the Albigenses, he wrote, had but an inkling of freedom, they ought to be praised most highly because they died for something that they themselves had not fully understood. In subsequent centuries, however, the "sunrise can no longer be hidden" behind scarlet capes and black cowls. The poem ends with the lines: "After the Albigenses followed the Hussites and paid back what the others had suffered. After Huss and Ziska came Luther, Hutten, the Thirty Years' War, the War of the Cevennes,[10] the conquerors of the Bastille, and so on." In tracing the quest for freedom from the Middle Ages to his own time, and leaving the end open, Lenau shifted from a religious to a political intent. The final words, an otherwise colorless "etc." have a special emphasis: the poem has a sting in its tail. The ending bespeaks Lenau's renewed interest in the liberal cause, but it does not add to the unity of the poem.

Die Albigenser interested the Young Germans, but it baffled Lenau's Swabian friends. Gustav Schwab was shocked that Lenau had turned Hegelian,[11] and Sophie Löwenthal prophesied that few women would enjoy reading the poem.[12] Those who had appreciated Lenau as a melancholic lyric poet were horrified. One wonders what Lenau's reaction was when a friend told him that a lady of the aristocracy in Munich, after reading half of *Die Albigenser,* burned the book "ceremoniously, while brewing coffee."[13] In its indefinite structure and arbitrary presentation, the poem has many shortcomings. Yet some of the rough-hewn fragments which make up the work have a monumentality that is found nowhere else in Lenau's work. The wide panorama they present points to seeds in Lenau's art which, had they been cultivated, would have added a new dimension to his predominantly lyric genius.

II Don Juan

In 1851, a year after Lenau's death, Anastasius Grün published a slim volume of the poet's posthumous works. It contained thirty-one poems which Lenau had not published for a variety of reasons; a very short dramatic fragment, *Helena,* concerned with the same legend that is treated in the chapbook about King Eginhard of Bohemia;[14] and the "dramatic poem" *Don Juan.*

Don Juan is usually classified as a fragment. Actually, Lenau completed the poem, as far as the main action is concerned, because Don Juan dies in the end. From comments of friends to whom Lenau had read the work, it may be concluded that they considered it finished. Yet Lenau—as with *Die Albigenser*—delayed submitting the manuscript to the publisher. His paralytic collapse interfered with all future plans. The manuscript remained in the hands of his close Stuttgart friends, the Reinbecks.

It is impossible to say to what extent Lenau himself had considered the work complete, and what revisions, if any, were planned. Little is known about the conception and execution of the work. In January, 1842, Lenau remarked to Max Löwenthal that he would like to write a *Don Juan*[15] which should differ from all existing versions. In March, 1844, he read to friends what he had then finished, and in May he wrote to Sophie that he was yearning for the "right mood in which to round off the scenes which are at present all too fragmentary" (V, 179). He had had the same misgivings about *Die Albigenser,* without subsequently making any changes in the manuscript. Early in September, amidst his attempts to collect papers necessary for his planned marriage to Maria Behrends, he wrote one more scene (V, 211). A few weeks later, on September 29, he suffered a light paralytic stroke, and in the night of October 12 he had his first paroxysm of insanity, during which he burned papers in a wash basin. The following morning he regretted the loss of his *Don Juan* manuscript—erroneously, as it turned out, because it was not among the burned papers. Emilie Reinbeck reportedly found it in a travel bag and put it aside.[16] On October 23, Lenau was committed to the insane asylum at Winnenthal.

To call *Don Juan* a fragment is misleading. The fact that the poem is considerably shorter than *Faust, Savonarola,* and *Die Albigenser* is of no consequence. Its episodic structure, depicting individual scenes without connecting them, is a feature that all Lenau's longer poems share. The poet may have revised a few clumsy lines and applied other finishing touches, if he had

had the opportunity. He might even have added a scene here and there, but not for any structural and thematic reasons. Unlike *Faust,* the poem is dramatic throughout, in the sense that the action is carried by the characters only. There are no epic interludes. Still, *Don Juan* is not a play. Like the dramatic portions of *Faust,* it consists of dialogues between the protagonist and an array of other characters who function only as vehicles for the hero's characterization but provide no dramatic element. Even the scenes with dynamic potential are static. The work is written in iambic pentameter, with a few passages in tetrameter. The rhyme schemes vary, heroic couplets being predominant.

Lenau's sources were Tirso de Molina's *El Burlador de Sevilla* (1630), the oldest Don Juan drama (which had appeared in a German translation in 1841), and Da Ponte's libretto to Mozart's opera, *Don Giovanni.* The fact that Byron[17] and Alfred de Musset[18] had written Don Juan poems was another reason for Lenau's strong interest in the theme.

If *Die Albigenser* signified Lenau's abjuration of mysticism, a turn toward the philosophy of Hegel, and a half-hearted endorsement of views held by David Friedrich Strauss and Heinrich Heine, *Don Juan* completes this development. Lenau had sworn to himself, while working on *Die Albigenser,* never to write another religious poem, but he kept the oath only partially. The subject-matter in *Don Juan,* to be sure, precludes theological debates, but Lenau's imagery derives, in part, from the religious realm. His protagonist is more than the libertine par excellence. He feels jealousy toward the women of all times who were either too old or too young to be conquered by him. His lustfulness exceeds the personal domain and manifests itself in expansive erotic images. Don Juan has found what all the Fausts in world literature have been seeking: the primordial principle of life, the heart of the universe:

> Das Herz, in dem die Wesen alle gründen,
> Der Born, worein sie sterbend alle münden,
> Der Gott der Zeugung ists, der Herr der Welt,
> Die er, nie satt, in seinen Armen hält.
> Nie wird in langer Brautnacht: Weltgeschichte
> Des Gottes Kraft, des Weibes Reiz zunichte;
> (II, 406-407)

("The heart in which all creatures live, the well into which they are emptied in death, it is the god of propagation, the lord of the world which he, never satiated, holds in his arms. The god's strength and the woman's desirability never fail during the long bridal night, which is world history.")

A god as the lover of the world, world history as the never ending bridal night—these images convey a primarily emotional attitude on the part of the poet, an attitude that has been called "unbounded paneroticism."[19] Sensualism is the basic outlook in *Don Juan,* and this outlook is given repeated poetic expression in images of religious fervor. In some passages the poem is reminiscent of Friedrich Schlegel's propagation of voluptuousness as a form of religion, and also of Heine's postulate of a religion of the flesh. Such phrases as *Götterleib* ([II, 424] godlike body) and *Gott der Freuden* ([II, 404] god of pleasures) abound, establishing connections between the spheres of physical sensuality and religious ecstasy. Don Juan exclaims "pleasure was my deity" (II, 440) and defines love as the "fiery breath of a god" (II, 442). Poetically, the work is very successful. The language is handled with great virtuosity and has a high musical quality.

Despite his ecstatic attitude, Don Juan is not a carefree libertine. The pursuit of pleasure is a serious, even grim endeavor to him. He is a pleasure-seeker without joy and essentially a woman hater. We see him either scheming about a future conquest with the woman pictured as the trapped victim, or, more frequently, cruelly breaking off a relationship. Don Juan's sensuality is rapacious; his love is marked by voracity and violence. His path is strewn with the corpses of mistresses and jealous rivals, and his savagery closely resembles that of Faust. In fact, the two characters and their adventures are so similar that many scenes could be interchanged between the works without any discrepancies showing.

In advocating sensualism as a *Weltanschauung* and even as a form of religion, Lenau turned against the concept of renunciation that he had observed both when writing *Savonarola* and in his relationship with Sophie. In *Don Juan,* he violently attacked all forms of asceticism, particularly celibacy. Sophie sensed the belligerence contained in the poem and was careful with her praise of the work which she had known in manuscript form. In a letter which she sent to Lenau at the Winnenthal asylum, six weeks after he had been committed, she said that she loved the poem but not the protagonist, because he uttered thoughts that would terrify her if they came from the poet's heart.[20] In one scene Don Juan subjects the monks of a monastery to a weird trick with the purpose of proving to them the unnaturalness of their vows. Wondering how the monks feel when the belling stag in the forest, the call of nature, awakens in them suppressed desires, he exclaims: "Oh sinister madness! wretched asceticism, while roundabout the warm pulse of God is beating!" (II, 407). To achieve his purpose, he smuggles into the monastery twelve wenches disguised as pages, then eagerly watches the monks' virtuousness crumble. He even professes to see a close link between religion and sensual fervor. The monks, he laughingly exclaims, are well-versed in the art of pious ecstasy; and therefore the fire of passion applied to real flesh and blood will be twice as intense. The joke develops beyond Don Juan's intentions. At the sight of the wicked scene, the abbot sets fire to the buildings and dies in the charred ruins.

No definite sequence in Don Juan's adventures is adhered to. One conquest follows another, some overlap. Don Juan's means to his ends include outright deception. In order to seduce Princess Isabella, he approaches her in a darkened room on the eve of her wedding day, pretending to be Fernando, her fiancé. Later after he has revealed his identity, he tells her of his philosophy: A woman can never love one particular man; she loves a dream image, an idea, and when she embraces a real person, he commits adultery against her image. "Even marriage is adultery," he concludes (II, 429).

Lenau uses imagery to associate Don Juan's sensuality with both religious sentiments and death. In the context of the poem, death appears, in the Romantic tradition of love-death, as a symbol of love's fullest realization. Don Juan expresses the sensation of supreme ecstasy through images of death. He wishes he could die in each union, then be reborn, with his heart perpetually rejuvenated, to pursue ever new delights (II, 447). Death appears as the highest principle of pleasure. But the protagonist is also associated with death in its concrete meaning. His love is destructive and brings death. The fact that many of Don Juan's conquests have perished lends him an aura of "fatal horror" (*Todesgrauen*) that makes him even more desirable in the eyes of some women. One lady, pondering a line of defense, wonders by what magical powers Don Juan makes her "yearn for the abyss that he is showing her" (II, 418). He visits a churchyard in order to renew his desire for pleasures by "imbibing the shudders of death" (II, 436). The embrace of a woman's body, the "epitome and the uttermost limit of heaven" (II, 424) is not love's true fulfillment to Don Juan. His desire aims for more:

> Möcht ich vergötternd ihn [ihren Leib] verderben,
> Mit ihr in eins zusammensterben.
>
> (II, 424)

("While deifying her body, I would like to destroy it and reach union with her in death.")

At this point, love-death and destruction are merged into one.

There is yet another association between Don Juan and the death-motif, one that is most characteristic of Lenau's protagonist and makes him unmistakably his own. Despite his libertinage, an awareness of transiency and death strongly contributes to Don Juan's psychological make-up. At times, his ecstasies of lust suddenly give way to desperate introspection, doubt, and hopelessness. In a conversation with his brother at the outset of the play, Don Juan tries to characterize the driving force behind his life. He feels as if there were something alien and wayward in his blood, an errant spirit from a different realm, a lost ferryman drifting in his veins, finding no place to stay, never gaining the "peace of a firm landing place" (II, 403).

Don Juan is caught in a dilemma. On the one hand, erotic pleasure is the essence of life to him; on the other, he questions the validity of that by which he lives. He is closely related to Faust, who eventually negated his own existence. In a comparison near the end of the poem, Don Juan denies the reality of love and conquest. During a dark night he saw the sky aglow with red splendor, as if a meteor were soaring through the air. Upon closer inspection, the phenomenon proved to be nothing but the reflection of a burning patch of rushes. After the reeds had turned to ashes, the sky was black again. Perhaps, Don Juan concludes, the magic of love is no more than that—merely a heavenly reflection of an earthbound fire. As soon as it dies down, the fanciful game is over (II, 442).

The analogy shows that the principles of materialism are no longer foreign to Lenau's thinking, and it also underscores the nature of Don Juan's death. In the older treatments of the theme, in Tirso de Molina's play, for example, Don Juan is punished for his licentious ways by a heavenly power. For Lenau, this power no longer existed. His place of damnation does not lie in the hereafter; it is in this world. In Lenau's eschatological thinking, every man carries his own hell within himself. Moreover, the protagonist did not commit any crimes, in Lenau's eyes, that would warrant punishment. He did not present Don Juan primarily as an evildoer. He regarded his hero as a paragon of that strength and ruthlessness which Lenau deeply admired. Much of *Don Juan* is the poet's wishful self-projection and is based on sentiments that could be investigated by a psychologist as profitably as by a literary historian. What brings about Don Juan's demise is the end of his strength, his inability to perpetuate his state of emotional ecstasy. This solution is uniquely Lenau's and makes the poem not only his most personal, confessional work, but also a document of an age which had ceased to subscribe to the moral and religious principles of German Idealism.

Don Juan does invite the "stone guest," the monument of a man he killed—an ancient motif connected with the Don Juan theme ever since Tirso de Molina. During the party which the statue is asked to attend, Don Juan suddenly feels a chill and suspects that the stone guest is near. His friend Marcello explains the chill away as a cold Don Juan may have caught in the drafty cemetery, but in the context of the poem it signifies more than that. The fire has died down, and the phantasmal ecstasies have ended. Once more, Don Juan voices his belief in the supremacy of physical pleasure and his desire to be like a stag pursuing a doe, but he feels betrayed by his own energy. "The flames of my blood have ceased to burn" (II, 439), he admits, then repeats the same thought in various metaphors. He was driven by a beautiful storm which has now abated (II, 441), and feels that his life, like a leaf, has faded and wilted (II, 438, 446, 447). His desires and his hopes are "stone dead" (II, 441).

In the final scene of the poem appears Don Pedro, the son of the man whose statue Don Juan had invited to the party. He has come to avenge his father's death and has brought with him a great number of women whose lives had been ruined by Don Juan, together with their offspring. Referred to by Don Juan as an "uncouth, ragged mob" (II, 443), they demand part of their seducer's wealth before Don Pedro runs him through. In a melancholic variation of Leporello's catalogue aria, Don Juan and his servant Catalinon[21] review a list of former mistresses, which serves as a testament at the same time. Don Juan has apportioned his wealth among the women whose names appear on the list and he asks Don Pedro to arrange execution of the testament. In the fencing duel, Don Juan proves to be an infinitely superior opponent, but he is determined to die. Humiliating his challenger, he inflicts many superficial injuries, chiding him with words as well. Only when Don Pedro appeals to him to end his suffering and deal him the finishing stroke does Don Juan cast his sword aside, leaving himself wholly vulnerable. "My mortal enemy is delivered into my hand; but this, too, is boresome, as is all of life" (II, 448). Then he receives the deadly thrust.

Don Juan, the poem which glorifies carnality, does not appear to some critics as an integral part of Lenau's work. They brush it aside as a tour de force in an area of imagination basically foreign to Lenau, a product of the incipient dementia. The latter assertion is partially true. A psychiatrist would easily detect in *Don Juan,* but also in *Die Albigenser,* symptoms characteristic of the early stages of general paralysis: a lack of balance and judgment; a deficiency in self-control; delusions of grandeur. Lenau's letters, written during the summer of 1844, show the same traits, but they also reveal his yet undiminished ability to observe himself soberly and to record in writing his fear of losing his mind. Aside from these pathological symptoms, the poem is very much Lenau's own, and in line with his other works. In his licentious hero, Lenau had found a symbol for aspects of his own nature: emotional ruthlessness and vehemence alternating with existential despair. When Don Juan's fierce prowess gives way to ennui and lethal fatigue, the poet's imagination is drawing on the same inner experiences he conveyed in the last "Waldlieder" and expressed in a letter to Sophie: the yearning for death, but a quiet and effortless death, "as if one lies down when one is very tired."

CHAPTER 8

Conclusion

THERE are two commonly held misconceptions about Lenau: that his phrenetic exploitation of his own sorrows through the medium of poetry finally brought on his mental collapse, making him a victim of his art; that his literary achievement constitutes the epitome of the *Weltschmerz* movement. In reality, his insanity was brought on through evident medical causes; it is a mistake to ascribe to it a deep, symbolical significance or to search for traces of insanity in his earlier works. And Lenau's relationship to the *Weltschmerz* movement was the same as Goethe's to the literature of the Storm and Stress period or as Walther's von der Vogelweide to the troubadour tradition, or as Hofmannsthal's to Impressionism. For a time, their work showed an affinity to the prevailing movement, but then the poets grew far beyond the limitations of a literary trend.

Lenau correctly observed that he had given everything to art. With good reason he called his personal life inconsequential and wasted. Surrounded mostly by mediocre people, he missed the stimulus as well as the criticism which artists usually gain from friendships with their peers. And yet, empty as his existence was, it became to Lenau the soil which nourished his imagination. He was not a poet of ideas. Too involved with his self and too impatient to follow at length a complex of abstract thought without relating it to himself, he relied on his psyche as almost the only source of poetic thought. In his long epic poems, Lenau did introduce philosophical and religious ideas, but the utter lack of continuity in their presentation and even their contradictory tendencies within a short period of time prove them to be mere vehicles for an underlying emotional attitude. Recently, East German and Hungarian scholars have tried to put Lenau on the pedestal of a political revolutionary and to make him a precursor of Marxism. They have re-evaluated his longer and shorter poems on the basis of inherent political messages they find exploitable for their own true or dictated political credo. Such attempts not only run contrary to all principles of serious literary scholarship—these critics are forced to close their eyes to every work that displeases them for entirely extra-literary reasons—but they do a great disservice to their champion: In the realm of politically inspired poems, Lenau was at his least original and most banal. Moreover, these poems are a far cry from Marxism.

Lenau was not a universal artist. Unlike the very greatest poets in world literature, he was not able to give voice to all emotions known to man. Only one specific category of inner experiences challenged his creativity, and along only one narrow line of impulses did his poetic genius grow: melancholy and despair. In creating verbal equivalents for these emotions, Lenau fulfilled his potential and achieved excellence. He did not strive toward any innovation of forms. The four-line rhymed stanza became his most important vehicle of expression. Other than Heine, who handled the same strophic form with detachment and irony, Lenau, who lacked Heine's humor and mental levity, used it with the serious fervor of a religious poet. But his religion knew of no hereafter, and his only belief was in man's misery.

Despite the limited range of his topics, Lenau's achievement as an artist is remarkable. Intellectually, he was rooted in an earlier period than most of his German contemporaries. The Austria of the early nineteenth century was steeped in rationalism. It had experienced no Romantic movement and had not partaken in the metaphysical irrationalism that swept Germany. It is characteristic of the literary traditions in the Austria of the 1820s that, two decades after the death of Novalis, Lenau chose Hölty as his literary model. A rational approach to the language was part of Lenau's poetic heritage. As a young, aspiring poet, and even on later occasions, he was fond of using cerebral comparisons in his verse. In keeping with his heritage, his imagination and his manner of thinking tended toward allegorical forms. And yet, in his own poetic career, Lenau left behind rationalism, passed through Romanticism, and created images and metaphors that point far beyond the traditions of the first half of the nineteenth century and are akin, in some respects, to the strongly symbolical language of modern literature.

New experiences in the world of reality did not affect his art. His treatment of nature shows best his subjective reaction to external impressions. To him, nature assumed significance only as a correlative to his emotions. In his poems it appears as a conveyor of human feelings. Although Lenau observed the external world closely and even with an eye for detail, he selected from all objects in nature those which best reflected his own mood. A group of gay nature poems, often artificial in tone, is vastly outnumbered by the melancholic. Lenau was prone to use images of nature animation, and he paid tribute to his rationalistic roots by drawing numerous parallels between the realms of man and of nature. But in his best poems the two are imperceptibly blended into a symbolic unity that conveys a mythical perception of nature reminiscent of that of Goethe or Novalis but in no way indebted to them. In his symbolical nature poems, Lenau established himself as one of the great lyrical poets in German literature.

Notes and References

Chapter 1

1. Eduard Castle (ed.), *Lenau und die Familie Löwenthal: Briefe und Gespräche, Gedichte und Entwürfe* (Leipzig, 1906), p. 157.

2. The only full-length biography on Lenau is still that by Anton X. Schurz, *Lenau's Leben,* 2 vols., (Stuttgart and Augsburg, 1855), a work justly called "equally useless and indispensable" by Eduard Castle, the foremost Lenau scholar. Castle began to prepare a new edition, but unfortunately it remained unfinished. For a good, if very brief, first-hand account of Lenau's life, see Anastasius Grün's introduction to his edition of the poet's work (Stuttgart, n.d. [1855]).

3. Schurz was the first to speak of her as a loose woman, and subsequent authors have outdone him in maligning her. For a fair judgment, see Heinrich Bischoff, *Nikolaus Lenaus Lyrik: Ihre Geschichte, Chronologie und Textkritik,* 2 vols. (Berlin, 1920-21).

4. The parenthetic references in the text refer to the standard edition of Lenau's works by Eduard Castle: *Sämtliche Werke und Briefe,* 6 vols. (Leipzig, 1910-1923). Vol. 1: Poems. Vol. 2: Longer epic and dramatic works. Vol. 3, 4, and 5: Letters and documents. Vol. 6: Critical apparatus.

5. For a detailed discussion of Lenau's relationship with the Swabian Poets, see Joseph Schick, *Nikolaus Lenau und die schwäbischen Dichter in ihren persönlichen, literarischen und dichterischen Beziehungen.* Strassburg (Diss.), 1908.

6. The most authoritative discussion of Lenau's trip to America is still George A. Mulfinger, "Lenau in Amerika." *Americana-Germanica I* (1897), No. 2, pp. 7-61; No. 3, pp. 1-16. The article contains valuable biographical source material.

7. It was situated in the Ohio Valley, across from the present town of Aliquippa. For a discussion of this society, see Karl J. Arndt, *George Rapp's Harmony Society, 1785-1847*. Philadelphia, 1965.

8. Cf. Mulfinger, No. 2, p. 51.

9. Emma Niendorf, *Lenau in Schwaben: Aus dem letzten Jahrzehnt seines Lebens* (Leipzig, 1855), p. 132.

10. J. Sadger, *Aus dem Liebesleben Nikolaus Lenaus. Schriften zur angewandten Seelenkunde,* ed. Siegmund Freud, vol. 6 (Leipzig and Vienna, 1909), pp. 4-11.

11. Vincenzo Errante, e.g., has compared them to Novalis' *Heinrich von Ofterdingen* (*Lenau: Geschichte eines Märtyrers der Poesie,* tr. Charlotte Rau, *[*Mengen, 1948*]*, p. 174).

12. Cf. Schurz II, 228. Lenau repeated the same thought to Schurz, while in the Winnenthal asylum (cf. *ibid.*, p. 246).

13. It is worth noting that Heine suffered a stroke in 1845, a year after Lenau, and was confined to bed for the eleven remaining years of his life. The *tabes dorsalis* from which he suffered had the same cause—syphilitic infection—as the *dementia paralytica* that beset Lenau.

Chapter 2

1. Schurz I, 71.
2. Cf. Bischoff I, 59ff.
3. "Das Kruzifix."
4. Johannes Hoffmeister (ed.), *Nachgoethesche Lyrik: Eichendorff, Lenau, Mörike.* Bonner Texte, vol. 3 (Bonn, 1948), pp. xixff.
5. "Ausgesetzt auf den Bergen des Herzens."
6. Cf. Wolfgang Martens, *Bild und Motiv im Weltschmerz: Studien zur Dichtung Lenaus.* Literatur und Leben, new series, ed. Richard Alewyn (Cologne and Graz, 1957), pp. 102-104; 120-123.
7. Martens, pp. 102-109.

Chapter 3

1. Georg Wilhelm Friedrich Hegel, *Sämtliche Werke,* ed. Hermann Glockner (Stuttgart, 1929), IX, 29-70 *passim.* (Introduction to Nature Philosophy)
2. Cf. Camillo von Klenze, *The Treatment of Nature in the Works of Nikolaus Lenau.* The Decennial Publications of the University of Chicago, first series, vol. 7 (Chicago, 1903), p. 6.
3. Castle, *Lenau-Löwenthal,* pp. 104-5.
4. Klenze, p. 79.
5. Ludwig August Frankl, *Zu Lenau's Biographie* (Vienna, 1854), p. 47.
6. Schurz I, 212.
7. In the first printing, the title was footnoted: "The unfortunate poet Mayrhofer." Johann Mayrhofer had committed suicide in 1836. Cf. VI, 434ff.
8. Cf. L. N. Reynaud, *N. Lenau: Poète lyrique* (Paris, 1904), p. 284.
9. Niendorf, pp. 14, 80.
10. Errante, p. 299.
11. For a full treatment of this theme, see Adelaide M. Weiss, *Merlin in German Literature: A Study of the Merlin Legend in German Literature from Medieval Beginnings to the End of Romanticism.* The Catholic University of America Studies in German, Vol. 3 (Washington, D.C., 1933.)

12. Hegel, IX, 48.

13. In German, *Kelch* also means "goblet, chalice" and carries strong poetic and religious connotations. The botanical error—moss does not have calyces—is less obvious in German since *Kelch* is a less scientific term than calyx.

Chapter 4

1. Cf. Anastasius Grün's introduction to his edition of Lenau's works (Stuttgart, 1855).

2. For a close examination of Lenau's images and motifs, see Wolfgang Martens, *op. cit.*

3. The Schwarzensee is near Bad Ischl, the Laudachsee near Gmunden, in the Austrian Salzkammergut.

4. Cf. Paul Weber, *America in Imaginative German Literature in the First Half of the Nineteenth Century* (New York, 1926), p. 103.

5. *Mein Leben* (Leipzig, 1813).

6. On the interpretation on "Primula Veris," however, see Karl J. Arndt in *The Germanic Review,* XXXIII (1958), 135-136.

7. Cf. Wagner-Scherzer, *Reisen in Nordamerika* (Leipzig, 1857), II,[2] 6.

8. Cf. Mulfinger, pp. 56-57.

9. Cf. Weber, p. 167-168.

10. It is not by accident that in this poem Lenau borrowed from another work that is representative of the attitude of his generation: Byron's *Manfred.* Cf. Siegfried Korninger, "Lord Byron und Nikolaus Lenau, eine vergleichende Studie." *English Miscellany,* III (1952), 70ff.

11. Cf. Karl Kurt Klein, "Ungarn in der deutschen Dichtung." *Deutsche Philologie im Aufriß,* ed. Wolfgang Stammler, III, (Berlin, 1962[2]), 557.

12. Schurz, II, 136.

13. *Grillparzers sämtliche Werke,* ed. Moritz Necker, (Leipzig, n.d. [1903]), XII, 105.

14. The official documents concerning these two cases are preserved in the *Haus-, Hof- und Staatsarchiv,* and in the *Archiv der Obersten Polizei- und Zensurstelle,* both in Vienna, and in various other archives. They are partly reprinted in Castle's Lenau edition. Cf. V, 118-199; VI, 630.

15. *Anastasius Grüns sämtliche Werke,* ed. Anton Schlossar (Leipzig, 1906), V, 128.

16. The poem was discovered by Karl J. Arndt and published in his essay "Lenau's Lost Poem 'An die Ultraliberalen in Deutschland' " in *The Germanic Review,* XIX (1944), 180-85.

17. Schurz, I, 224.

Chapter 5

1. There were controversies between the Kings of France and Poland during Richelieu's term of office, and John Casimir did live in France before he was summoned to the throne of Poland in 1648. He held the position of a cardinal. As John II, he was King of Poland from 1648 to 1668, the last of the Polish Vasas. In 1672, after having been deposed, he married a French adventuress, Claudine Françoise [commonly: Marie] Mignot (c. 1617-1711). He died a few weeks later. The story of Marie Mignot's life, though much modified, was the subject of a "vaudeville" play by Antoine Bayard and Paul Duport, *Marie Mignot* (1829). The source of Oppeln-Bronikowski's novel, published two years earlier, is not known.

2. It is conceivable that Lenau saw a puppet play based on the *Spanish Tragedy* as a child, an experience comparable to Goethe's first contact with the Faust legend. If true, this would explain his associating the theme with the puppet motif.

3. "Mischka" is Hungarian for "Michael." The Theiss (Hung.: Tisza) and the Marosch (Maros) are rivers in Hungary.

4. For a critical survey, see Johannes Bolte, "Lenaus Gedicht *Anna*". *Euphorion,* IV (1897), 323-333.

5. In his poem, Lenau used the standard German form, Ziska, of the name.

Chapter 6

1. Cf. Julius Petersen, "Faustdichtungen nach Goethe." *Deutsche Vierteljahrsschrift für Literaturwissenschaft und Geistesgeschichte,* XIV (1936), 474.

2. Lenau had read it in the more recent version of Nikolaus Pfitzer, 1674.

3. For the following, also cf. Hugo Schmidt, "Religious Issues and Images in Lenau's Works," in *The Germanic Review,* XXXIX (1964), 163-182.

4. For a tracing of sources in Lenau's poem, see August Hildebrand, "Lenaus *Faust.*" *Neue Jahrbücher für das klassische Altertum, Geschichte und deutsche Literatur,* XIX (1907), 41-73.

5. Karl Gutzkow, *Beiträge zur Geschichte der neuesten Literatur* (Stuttgart, 1836), I, 131-142. Gutzkow called *Faust* "a complete failure," and the protagonist "a shadow and a figure without consequence." Theodor Mundt and Karl Laube followed suit. Cf. Bischoff I, 573-574.

6. Cf. Harald Höffding, *Sören Kierkegaard als Philosoph* (Stuttgart, 1896), pp. 18ff.

7. Cf. Walter Lowrie, *Kierkegaard* (London, 1938), pp. 504-509, *passim.*

8. The following lines were added in the second edition: 167-174;

269-354; 680-697; 712-715; 752-775; 1831-1834; 2181-2182; 2197-2200; 2243-2250; 2311-2316; 2325-2452; 2469-2470; 2977-2980; 3052-3055; 3286-3303. Some forty lines from the first edition were deleted in the second—mostly for esthetic reasons, it would seem—and a few passages were rearranged. It should be noted that a year before the first edition Lenau published a large fragment of his *Faust* (up to II, 95) in the *Frühlingsalmanach* edited by him.

9. Cf. Carl Siegel, "Lenaus *Faust* und sein Verhältnis zur Philosophie." *Kant-Studien,* XXI (1916), 66-92.

10. Karl Meier, *Girolamo Savonarola, aus großen Theils handschriftlichen Quellen dargestellt* (Berlin, 1836); Ludwig Flathe, *Geschichte der Vorläufer der Reformation.* 2 vols. (Leipzig, 1835); Wilhelm Roscoe, *Lorenz von Medici,* tr. Kurt Sprengel (Berlin, 1797, and Vienna, 1817). According to a note to Sophie, Lenau also consulted Savonarola's writings (cf. IV, 51).

11. Errante, p. 199. In connection with Errante's unbounded admiration for Lenau, a small misunderstanding should be pointed out. Errante is often criticized for calling Lenau "Europe's greatest lyrical poet" (*der größte europäische Lyriker,* p. 156). This is an error on the part of the translator of Errante's book into German. The Italian originial merely states that Lenau is "uno dei piú grandi lirici non solo tedeschi ma europei."

12. Castle suspects that Lenau set a monument to his friendship with Martensen in this scene. Cf. Eduard Castle, "Nikolaus Lenaus *Savonarola.*" *Euphorion,* IV (1897), 73.

13. Josef Nadler, *Geschichte der deutschen Literatur* (Vienna, 1951), p. 613.

14. *Goethes Werke* (Weimar edition), sect. IV, vol. IL (1909), 102.

15. Cf. e.g., *Nikolaus Lenaus Briefe an einen Freund: Herausgegeben mit Erinnerungen an den Verstorbenen von Karl Mayer* (Stuttgart, 1853), p. 179.

16. *Heinrich Heines sämtliche Werke* (ed. Ernst Elster), Leipzig, n.d. *[1887ff.]*), IV, 246.

17. Cf. Castle, *Euphorion,* III, 72.

18. *Ernst Freiherrn von Feuchterslebens sämtliche Werke,* ed. Friedrich Hebbel, 7 vols. (Vienna, 1851-1853), IV, 105.

19. No. 132 (December 29, 1837).

20. No. 39 (March, 1838), pp. 305-308.

21. *Deutsche Dichtung* (Stuttgart, 1858-1859), III, 475-476.

22. *Nikolaus Lenau, seine Ansichten und Tendenzen mit besonderer Hindeutung auf sein neuestes Werk "Savonarola"* (Hamburg, 1838).

23. *Aus meinem Leben,* tr. A. Michelsen. 2 vols. (Heidelberg, 1883), I, 216.

Chapter 7

1. The Manichaean doctrine of the Two Principles also underlies Byron's biblical "mystery," *Cain* (1821).

2. Castle, Lenau-Löwenthal, p. 104.

3. Other sources were P. F. Stuhr, *Allgemeine Geschichte der Religionsformen der heidnischen Völker* (Berlin, 1836-1838); Friedrich von Raumer, *Geschichte der Hohenstaufen und ihrer Zeit* (Reutlingen, 1828-1829); Ferdinand Christian Baur, *Die christliche Gnosis oder die christliche Religions-Philosophie in ihrer geschichtlichen Entwicklung* (Tübingen, 1835); Friedrich Diez, *Leben und Werke der Troubadours* (Zwickau, 1829). Besides these, Lenau used two primary sources. One was Michel-Jean-Joseph Brial, *Recueil des Historiens des Gaules et de la France,* vol. 19, ed. J. Naudet and P.Cl.Fr. Daunou (Paris, 1833); the other was the recently discovered Provençal poem on the Albigensian Wars, *Histoire de la Croisade contre les hérétiques Albigeois, écrite en vers provençaux par une poëte contemporain,* edited with a translation into modern French by Claude Fauriel, in the *Collection de Documents inédits sur l'histoire de France,* first series, vol. 12 (Paris, 1837).

4. Castle, Lenau-Löwenthal, p. 104-105.

5. *Ibid.*, p. 231.

6. *Histoire de la Croisade contre les hérétiques Albigeois.*

7. Lenau's source for this image came from Indian mythology. He found it in Stuhr, I, 108.

8. Hegel XI, 25-157, *passim* (Introduction to the Philosophy of History).

9. *Ibid.*, VII, 436 (Philosophy of Right).

10. A religious war in southern France, 1702-1705, brought on through the revocation of the Edict of Nantes.

11. *Justinus Kerners Briefwechsel mit seinen Freunden,* ed. Th. Kerner and E. Müller (Stuttgart and Leipzig, 1897), No. 573.

12. Castle, Lenau-Löwenthal, p. 112.

13. Niendorf, pp. 169-170.

14. Cf. Joseph Görres, *Die teutschen Volksbücher* (Heidelberg, 1807), pp. 85-90.

15. Castle, Lenau-Löwenthal, p. 210.

16. Niendorf, p. 262; Schurz, II, 224.

17. *Don Juan,* 1819-1824.

18. "Namouna," 1832, and *Une Matinée de Don Juan,* 1833.

19. József Turóczi-Trostler, *Lenau,* tr. Bruno Heilig (Neue Beiträge zur Literaturwissenschaft, ed. W. Krauss and H. Mayer [Berlin, 1961]), p. 251.

20. Castle, Lenau-Löwenthal, p. 332.

21. Lenau borrowed the servant's name from Tirso de Molina's play.

Selected Bibliography

PRIMARY SOURCES

NIKOLAUS LENAU, *Sämtliche Werke und Briefe*, ed. Eduard Castle, 6 vols. (Leipzig, 1910-1923). Vol. 1: Poems. Vol. 2: Longer epic and dramatic works. Vols. 3, 4, and 5: Letters and documents. Vol. 6: Critical apparatus. The critical standard edition of Lenau's works and letters and a masterpiece of scholarly editing.

NIKOLAUS LENAU, *Sämtliche Werke und Briefe*, ed. Hermann Engelhard (Stuttgart, 1959). A handy edition of the complete works, and a selection of the letters.

Poems and Letters of Nikolaus Lenau, translated, with an introduction, by Winthrop H. Root (New York, 1964). A selection of Lenau's poems with English verse translations on facing pages. Also contains a selection of the poet's notes to Sophie. The only English translation of poems by Lenau in book form. Very successful in part.

SECONDARY SOURCES

A. Biographical:

AUERBACH, BERTHOLD, *Nikolaus Lenau. Erinnerungen und Betrachtungen* (Vienna, 1876). Recollections by a fellow writer.

BUCHOWIECKI, JOSEF (ed.), *Nikolaus Lenau: Briefwechsel. Unveröffenlichtes und Unbekanntes* (Vienna, 1969). Fifty-four unpublished letters from and to Lenau, and several poems.

CASTLE, EDUARD, *Lenau und die Familie Löwenthal: Briefe und Gespräche, Gedichte und Entwürfe* (Leipzig, 1906). Contains material pertinent to a study of Lenau's relationship to Sophie Löwenthal.

FRANKL, LUDWIG AUGUST, *Zur Biographie Nikolaus Lenaus* (Vienna, 1854, second edition, 1885). Recollections by a friend of Lenau's.

GRÜN, ANASTASIUS, "Nikolaus Lenau. Lebensgeschichtliche Umrisse." The introduction on Lenau's life in Grün's edition, Stuttgart, n.d. [1855].

HÄRTLING, PETER (ed.), *Nikolaus Lenau: Briefe an Sophie von Löwenthal (1834-1845)* (Munich, 1968). A very handsome edition, incl. an introduction and well-prepared critical material.

MAYER, KARL, *Nikolaus Lenau's Briefe an einen Freund*, herausgegeben mit Erinnerungen an den Verstorbenen von Karl Mayer

(Stuttgart, 1853). Contains recollections of Lenau by the Swabian Poet.

Minckwitz, Friedrich, *Nikolaus Lenau und Sophie Löwenthal. Briefe und Tagebücher* (Weimar, 1963). Does not add any new material to Castle's *Lenau und die Familie Löwenthal* (1906).

Niendorf, Emma (pseud. Emma von Suckow), *Lenau in Schwaben. Aus dem letzten Jahrzehnt seines Lebens* (Leipzig, 1855). Recollections by a friend.

Obermayer, Eugene, "Erinnerungen an Lenau." *Österreichisches Jahrbuch,* 1888, pp. 239-253. Not always reliable, especially with regard to dates.

Pauker, Wolfgang, *Lenaus Freundin Nanette Wolf in Gmunden* (Vienna & Leipzig, 1923). A meticulous and valuable study on the life of a friend of Lenau's and the poet's relationship to her.

Schlossar, Anton, *Nikolaus Lenaus Briefe an Emilie von Reinbeck und deren Gatten Georg von Reinbeck 1832-1844, nebst Emilie von Reinbecks Aufzeichnungen über Lenaus Erkrankung 1844-1846 nach den großentheils ungedruckten Originalen herausgegeben von Dr. Anton Schossar* (Stuttgart, 1896). Interesting record of Lenau's incipient insanity.

Schurz, Anton X., *Lenau's Leben, großentheils aus des Dichters eigenen Briefen.* 2 vols. (Stuttgart & Augsburg, 1855). Still the only full-length biography of Lenau, and as such completely inadequate. It was renewed and re-edited by Eduard Castle, but unfortunately only one volume, covering the years 1798-1831, appeared (Vienna, 1913).

Weisser, Paul (ed.), "Lenau und Marie Behrends: Aufzeichnungen der Braut Lenaus und Briefe des Dichters an sie." *Deutsche Rundschau,* LXI (1889), 420-450. Recollections of Lenau's fiancée.

B. Critical Studies:

Anderson, George K., *The Legend of the Wandering Jew* (Providence, 1965). An exemplary, exhaustive treatment of the motif.

Arndt, Karl J. R., "The Effect of America on Lenau's Life and Work." *The Germanic Review,* XXXIII (1958), 125-142. Stresses the religious experience.

Bischoff, Heinrich, *Nikolaus Lenaus Lyrik: Ihre Geschichte, Chronologie und Textkritik.* Vol. 1: Geschichte der lyrischen Gedichte von N. Lenau. Vol. 2: Chronologie und Textkritik. Mit einem Anhang: Tagebuch von Max Löwenthal (Berlin, 1921). Next to Castle's edition, the most valuable contribution to Lenau criticism. The first volume (of over 800 pages) places each of Lenau's poems into its biographical context and traces all influences to which Lenau was exposed. The second volume contains biographical material not covered by Castle in his *Lenau und die Familie Löwenthal.*

Blankenagel, John C., "Deeds to Lenau's Property in Ohio." *The Germanic Review,* II (1927), 202-212.

Britz, Nikolaus (ed.), *Lenau-Almanach* (Vienna). This almanack appeared in two volumes, 1963/64 and 1965/66. It offers articles on Lenau by various scholars, as well as reports on the annual meetings of the "Internationale Lenau-Gesellschaft." In 1969, it was superseded by the quarterly, *Lenau-Forum* (ed. N. Britz, Vienna).

Castle, Eduard, "Amerikamüde: Lenau und Kürnberger." *Jahrbuch der Grillparzergesellschaft,* XII (1906), 15-42. Lenau's American sojourn in its importance for Kürnberger's novel, *Der Amerikamüde* (1856).

———. *Nikolaus Lenau: Zur Jahrhundertfeier seiner Geburt.* Leipzig, 1902. (A brief, authoritative monograph.)

———. "Nikolaus Lenaus *Savonarola.*" *Euphorion,* III (1896), 74-92; 441-464; IV (1897), 66-91.

Deutsch, Johannes, *Zur Psychologie und Ästhetik der Lyrik: Untersuchungen an Lenau* (Greifswald, 1914). Detailed examination of a few poems.

Errante, Vincenzo, *Lenau. Storia di un martire della poesia* (Milan & Messina, 1935). A comprehensive study of Lenau's works, marred by a lack of scholarly restraint. The German translation (by Charlotte Rau, Mengen, 1948) is full of errors and quite unreadable.

Greven, E., *Die Naturschilderung in den Dichtwerken von Nikolaus Lenau* (Strassburg, 1910).

Hildebrand, August, "Lenaus *Faust.*" *Neue Jahrbücher für das klassische Altertum, Geschichte und deutsche Literatur,* X (1907), 41-73. A general discussion, and a tracing of influences.

Klenze, Camillo von, *The Treatment of Nature in the Works of Nikolaus Lenau.* The Decennial Publications of the University of Chicago. 1st series, vol. 7 (Chicago, 1903) pp. 27-109.

Korninger, Siegfried, "Lord Byron und Nikolaus Lenau: Eine vergleichende Studie." *English Miscellany,* III (1952), 61-123. An illuminating comparison of motifs.

Korr, Anton, *Lenaus Stellung zur Naturphilosophie* (Münster, 1914).

Krueger, P., "Lenaus *Albigenser* und ihre Quellenschriften." Wissenschaftliche Beilage zum Programm der Luisenstädtischen Oberrealschule (Berlin, 1886).

Martens, Wolfgang, *Bild und Motiv im Weltschmerz: Studien zur Dichtung Lenaus. Literatur und Leben,* new series, vol. 4 (Cologne & Graz, 1957). A study of Lenau's use of images and motifs, with emphasis on Existentialist ideas.

MULFINGER, GEORGE A., "Lenau in Amerika." *Americana-Germanica.* I (1897), No. 2, pp. 7-61; No. 3, pp. 1-16. The most authoritative discussion of Lenau's journey to America. Contains some biographical source material.

NEUMANN, GERHARD, "Das 'Vergänglich Bild'. Untersuchungen zu Lenaus lyrischem Verfahren." *Zeitschrift für deutsche Philologie,* LXXXVI (1967), 485-509. This incisive study appeared after the present manuscript had been completed. In summary, Neumann says that Lenau's poems do not represent nature; they withdraw into their own language, a language that no longer represents its object, and yet remains realistic and conventional. Lenau's language has become inadequate as a vehicle, and his imagery points far into the future.

RASCH, WOLFDIETRICH, "Nikolaus Lenaus Doppelsonett 'Einsamkeit.'" *Deutsche Vierteljahrsschrift für Literaturwissenschaft und Geistesgeschichte,* XXV (1951), 214-231.

REYNAUD, L. N., *N. Lenau: Poète lyrique* (Paris, 1904). An early comprehensive study of Lenau's poems.

ROUSTAN, L., *Lenau et son temps* (Paris, 1898). One of the more important early studies of Lenau.

SADGER, J., *Aus dem Liebesleben Nikolaus Lenaus. Schriften zur angewandten Seelenkunde,* ed. Siegmund Freud, vol. 6. (Leipzig & Vienna, 1909). A psychoanalytic study, dubious in its methods and conclusions, but of some interest.

SCHAERFFENBERG, MAX, *Nikolaus Lenaus Dichterwerk als Spiegel der Zeit.* Ein Beitrag zur religiösen Geistesgeschichte des dritten bis fünften Jahrzehnts des neunzehnten Jahrhunderts. Erlanger Arbeiten zur deutschen Literatur, vol. 3 (Erlangen, 1935). A thorough and scholarly study.

SCHICK, JOSEPH, *Nikolaus Lenau und die schwäbischen Dichter in ihren persönlichen, literarischen und dichterischen Beziehungen* (Strassburg, 1908).

SCHMIDT, HUGO, "Religious Issues and Images in Lenau's Works." *The Germanic Review,* XXXIX (1964), 163-182. Mostly about Lenau's longer epic-dramatic poems.

———. "Natursymbole in Nikolaus Lenaus Gedichten." *Lenau-Almanach,* 1963/64, 46-72. A theoretically oriented discussion of Lenau's nature symbolism.

SCHNEIDER, REINHOLD, "Der Katarakt: Lenaus geistiges Schicksal." *Über Dichter und Dichtung* (Cologne, 1953), p. 11-46. A general essay on Lenau.

SIEGEL, CARL, "Lenaus *Faust* und sein Verhältnis zur Philosophie." *Kant-Studien,* XXI (1916), 66-92.

STAMM, ISRAEL, "Lenau's *Faust.*" *Germanic Review,* XXVI (1951), 5-12.

THORSLEV, PETER L., *The Byronic Hero: Types and Prototypes* (Minneapolis, 1962). Includes discussions on the Faust and Ahasuerus figures in European literature.

TURÓCZI-TROSTLER, JÓZSEF, *Lenau* (Budapest, 1955), tr. Bruno Heilig (Berlin, 1961) (*Neue Beiträge zur Literaturwissenschaft,* vol. 12). An attempt by a Marxist critic to relate Lenau's works to the forces of social unrest and revolt in the nineteenth century. A strongly biased, poorly documented piece of work.

VAN HESSEN, JOZEF, *Nicolaus Lenau und das Junge Deutschland* (Gravenhage, n.d. [1925]).

WALZEL, OSKAR, "Nikolaus Lenau." *Vom Geistesleben des 18. und 19. Jahrhunderts* (Leipzig, 1911), pp. 330-377. A good general discussion.

WEGE, LISELOTTE, *Hegel und Lenau* (Dresden, 1932).

WEHNER, JOHANNA, *Lenaus literarisches Verhältnis zu Friedrich Matthisson* (Münster, 1914).

WEISS, WALTER, "Heines, Lenaus und Immermanns Kritik am Pantheismus." *Germanistische Abhandlungen,* ed. Karl K. Klein and Eugen Turnherr, Innsbruck, 1959, pp. 191-221.

———, "Nikolaus Lenau." *Enttäuschter Pantheismus. Zur Weltgestaltung der Dichtung in der Restaurationszeit* (Dornbirn, 1962), pp. 67-122. (Vol. 3 of *Gesetz und Wandel,* ed. K. K. Klein and E. Turnherr.) Concerned with Lenau's attitudes to pantheism.

Index

B. Works